A. C. (Arthur Coke) Burnell

The Vamcabrahmana

Being the eighth Brahmana of the Sama Veda

A. C. (Arthur Coke) Burnell

The Vamcabrahmana
Being the eighth Brahmana of the Sama Veda

ISBN/EAN: 9783741142338

Manufactured in Europe, USA, Canada, Australia, Japa

Cover: Foto ©Thomas Meinert / pixelio.de

Manufactured and distributed by brebook publishing software
(www.brebook.com)

A. C. (Arthur Coke) Burnell

The Vamcabrahmana

THE

VAṂÇABRĀHMAṆA

(BEING THE EIGHTH BRĀHMAṆA)

OF THE

SĀMA VEDA

EDITED TOGETHER WITH THE COMMENTARY OF SĀYAṆA
A PREFACE AND INDEX OF WORDS

BY

A. C. BURNELL, M. R. A. S.
etc. etc.

MANGALORE
PRINTED BY STOLZ & HIRNER, BASEL MISSION PRESS
1873

(100 Copies)

TO

Dr. VIGGO FAUSBOELL

"WHO DIVIDES WITH THE ILLUSTRIOUS BURNOUF THE FAME OF HAVING CREATED PALI SCHOLARSHIP"

This is affectionately inscribed

BY HIS OLD FRIEND AND PUPIL

A. BURNELL

PREFACE.

In printing Sâyana's Commentaries on the lesser Brâhmanas of the Sâma Veda, I am induced to include that on the Vamçabrâhmana, not because I consider that it is in any way worthy of his name, but because I consider that whatever the representative man of modern Sanskrit literature in India has issued must be of some historical interest. The revival of Vedic studies in India appears to have commenced about 800 A. D. and to have lasted not much beyond 1500; and the one great name in connection with that movement is Sâyana's. There are Treatises and Commentaries of a much later date, but they are nearly always diffuse compilations by mere pedants, whereas Sâyana (except in a few details) gives a most judicious summary of all that was known to the Brahmans at the middle and end of the 14th century A. D. when these studies had not yet ceased to possess a living interest. In the mirage-chronology of India every certain date is of importance and his date is as certain as it well can be.

I.

Much as Sâyana's works have been criticized, and though many have been edited in a way that leaves nothing to be desired, it is by no means easy to find a satisfactory account of the writer. It has generally been held that Bukka king of Vidyânagara in the 14th century A. D. had a minister named Mâdhava to whom and to whose younger brother Sâyana the great commentaries on the Vedas and many other treatises are to be ascribed. Almost every Sanskritist tells a different tale.* That these works were composed under Bukka, the prefaces show; and the names of Mâdhava and Sâyana seemed clearly to indicate that a passage which speaks of Sâyana as Mâdhava's younger brother could only mean that and nothing more. A third name which occurs in the MSS.—Vidyâranyasvâmin—was slurred over; it is however the key to the solution of the difficulty. That these three names belong to one and the same person, the following details of his life will show.

At the beginning of the 14th century A. D. the Muhammadan invaders of India had reduced all the North, and it only remained for them to conquer the Deccan; this they did in a very short period, chiefly owing to the treachery and internal trouble existing in the southern kingdoms. They met however with considerable resistance from two states which comprised greater part of the Telugu and Canarese country, and which had their capitals in Devagiri and Varangal. The former fell in 1307; the latter (by far the more remarkable in the history of S. Indian civilization) in March 1310†. For some time before 1292 (or 1295) this kingdom had been ruled by a widowed queen Rudramma Devî (a Devagiri Princes),

* Following the chronological order we have Colebrooke (Essays I., 301), who mentions Sâyana as a brother of Mâdhava, and (do: p. 53) Vidyâranya as Mâdhava's preceptor.

Wilkes's "Mysore" (i. p. 153 and note) says that Vidyâranya's *former* name was Mâdhavâcârya.

Lassen I. A. K. iv. p. 171. "Bukkarâja's berühmter erster minister Mâdhavâcârja, mit dem beinamen Vidjâranja;" again (p. 172) "Mâdhava und sein bruder Sâjana" and (p. 178, n.) "Mâdhava dessen lehrer Vidjâranja biess." Roth (in Z. d. d. M. G. xxi., p. 8.) repeats the assertion that there were *two* brothers. So Dr. Bhau Dâjî (in Bombay As. S. J. viii. 225-8).

† Amîr Khusrû (in *Sir H. Elliot's* History of India, by Dowson, iii. p. 84.)

who seems to have entirely gained the affections of her people;* she resigned in favour of her son Pratâpa Rudra Deva, whose family-name was Kâkatêya.† This king, though certainly a Dravidian, seems to have been a devout Hindu, and a great patron of Sanskrit literature, but in accordance with the gross habits of flattery of the country and time, the works he patronized appear in his own name, and not in that of the real author. Of all the compilations (for they are nothing more) that he issued, the best known is perhaps a treatise on law, the Sarasvatîvilâsa. The Telugu people was not long introduced to Brahmanism and had all the zeal of new converts; thus the Brahmans effected their object of establishing a priestly tyranny with the greatest ease. This form of Government would, no doubt, have effected much more had it not come too late. As it was, its powers to amalgamate half savage tribes had hardly a fair trial in Central and S. India, and it was ruined by invasion before complete results could become apparent. In these troubled times Sâyana was born. His family, tradition says, was originally settled on the banks of

* Cfr. *Marco Polo*, by *Col. Yule* II., 295-7.

† Explained by one Commentator (Kumârasvâmin) as derived from the name of a local form of Durgâ. As this writer is a son of Kolâcala Mallinâtha the well known Commentator on the poems attributed to Kâlidâsa, these Commentaries cannot be earlier than the 14th century, and represent the Varangal revival of Sanskrit studies in the direction of polite literature and poetry as opposed to the Vedic and Philosophic studies pursued at Vidyânagara.

I may take this opportunity of protesting against Lassen's restorations of the former and of other names in Southern India. He takes Dravidian words transcribed without system, and then endeavours to make out of them some Sanskrit word or other, sense or nonsense. In his map one finds Aranyakonda given as the ancient name of Varangal; this last is a *Muhammadan* and corrupt way of writing Orukkal which is translated in Sanskrit books that mention the place by Ekaçaila, both meaning "One-rock." Aranyakonda is nonsense, and there is not the least trace of such a name!

the Krish*n*a, but his father had fled to Hampe afterwards called Vijayanagara or Vidyânagara.* They were Telugu Brahmans claiming descent from Bharadvâja and his father was *perhaps* called Mayana. If tradition is right (as it very likely is), in making Sâya*n*a thirty-six years of age when he renounced the world, his birth must have occurred in 1295. His family professed the Black Yajur Veda, and used the Baudhâyana-sûtra, and were, no doubt, priests by profession. This Black Yajur Veda is peculiarly the Veda of the Telugu Brahmans, and it was formerly studied so much in their settlements on the banks of the Krish*n*a and Godâvarî that an old Telugu proverb says: "There even the house-cats know the Yajur Veda." Hampe became a sort of city of refuge for fugitives from the Muhammadans,† and some low caste cowherds rose to power chiefly through Maya*n*a's influence who opportunely discovered that they were descended from the Lunar race (Somavamça), and became the spiritual and therefore temporal adviser of this family. He was certainly not justified in doing so by the strict letter of his law, but the arrangement was otherwise good and prudent.‡

---

*This place is said to have had no less than nine different names, (see Brown's "Cyclic Tables" Edn. of 1850 p. 56) viz: *A*pê or Hampe; Nâgarka*tt*u; *A*nêgondi; Pampâxetram; Vidyânagara; Jayapura; Pâ*nd*avavijayâpura; Vijayanagara; Râyapa*tt*anam. As the Muhammadan historians who were contemporaneous with the early days of this kingdom write the name "Bijânagar," it is probable that Vidyânagara is more correct than Vijayanagara.

†The site of the town is in a barren and inaccessible part of the Deccan, which is perhaps the driest and most barren part of S. India.

‡Vulgar tradition attributes the foundation of Vidyânagara to him or rather to Sâya*n*a himself, and to the use he made of a hidden treasure, but the place seems to have existed before their time.

Sâyana* was probably an only surviving child. In the East the superstition of the evil eye and of malignant spirits is universal, and its effects are to be noticed in the minutest details of life. If parents in S. India repeatedly lose children

* That Mâdhavâcârya adopted the name of Vidyâranyasvâmin on becoming a Sannyâsin is stated in the Çringêri list and is universally allowed since Dr. Hall's identification ("Contributions towards an Index to the Bibliography of the Indian Philosophical Systems"); Colebrooke's statement that Vidyâranya was Mâdhavâcârya's *preceptor* (Essays I., 23) is owing to an oversight, as I have never been able to find anything which warrants it.* That Sâyana is merely another name of the same person appears from the following reasons:—

1. In the Parâçarasmrítivyâkhyâ Mâdhava says of his descent and family:

çrîmatî Jananî yasya sukîrtir Mâyanah pitâ, |
Sâyano bhoganâthaç ca, manobuddhî sahodarau ‖ 6 ‖
yasya Baudhâyanam sûtram, çâkhâ yasya ca yâjushî |
bhâradvâjakulam yasya sarvajnah sa hi Mâdhavah ‖ 7 ‖

[Aufrecht "Catalogus" p. 264, a. supported by MSS. from all parts of India, *e. g.* Tanjore 519 (N. Indian); do. 9,225 and 9,226 (grantha) and 9,227 (Telugu).] These lines are quite intelligible except the second. It is evident that the construction is the same throughout and that therefore this must be explained: "(yasya) bhoganâthah Sâyano (yasya) ca sahodarau manobuddhî"—(whose) bhoganâtha (is) Sâyana and (whose) brothers (are) Manas and Buddhi. Now bhoganâtha is certainly not a proper name, and never could be taken as such by any one at all acquainted with the Indian practice as regards names. It is enough to point out that a single instance of this word being used as a proper name elsewhere does not occur; it must, therefore, be taken as an attributive, as the construction requires, and its explanation is furnished by the Vedânta system. Sâyana's "Pancadaçî" is full of such allegories, and he is in this respect far more original than most Indians. The Vedânta system, as is well known, acknowledges only one permanent substance—Brahma; by the action of illusion (mâyâ) on this substance are produced all the objects which have only a practical (Vyâvahârika) existence as opposed to the real (Pâramârthika) existence of Brahma, and which are composed of combinations in various proportions of the Mahâbhûta or elements. Of the corporeal part of men such is the existence; it is not real, but serves

* The Parâçarasmrítivyâkhyâ which is said expressly (in its preface) to have been composed by Mâdhava is quoted as the work of Vidyâranyasvâmin in the Viramitrodaya (about 1550-1600) 209. a. l. 10 (of the original edition). As regards the date of this work, v. West and Bühler's "Digest," I., p. x.

in their infancy, they give the next child born to them a name to propitiate the evil influences that have (they think) destroyed the others, and Sâyana is one of these names used by the Telugus. It signifies "Mortal" and is a pure Dravidian word, but properly Sâyanna; anna (= elder brother) being an

as a temporary means to punish souls for their ignorance which results in works, and as such (sthûla and sûxma çarîra) is called Bhogâyatanam or Bhogasâdhanam "the abode of" and "means to" sensual impressions; Bhoganâtha is the same but personified. Sâyana is therefore the Bhoganâtha or mortal body of Mâdhava the soul identified with Vishnu who is (as Dr. Hall has rightly shown*) the supreme Brahma of the followers of Çankarâcârya and of whom Mâdhava is a name. The Vedic Commentaries are a good work of the better part of the author, and are therefore "Mâdhavîya" belonging to or dedicated to Mâdhava; but Sâyana or the mortal body actually writes them, and is ordered by the king Bukka to do so. Manas and Buddhi are his brothers being the perceptive and reasoning faculties born with him. It must also be remarked that Mâyana is probably not his father's real name, as Çrîmatî is certainly not his mother's. (cfr. Bombay A. S. J. ix. p. 228 and the extract from Devarâja below.)

2. This explanation is fully borne out by Canndappa's remark in his preface to the Âpastambaprayogaratnamâlâ. He was minister to Vîrabhûpati (who reigned at Vidyânagara from about 1418-1434), and most probably was personally acquainted with Vidyâranyasvâmin. The only MSS. of this work which I know of (at Tanjore) unfortunately all have a lacuna in the first part of the seventh çloka which runs:

Vedân vyâkhyân Mâdhavâryaḥ Sâyanâryavapurdharaḥ ||

or—"Mâdhava (the soul) embodied in Sâyana commented on the Vedas." No other explanation of Vapurdharaḥ is possible.

3. In his preface to the Sarvadarçanasangraha it is said:

çrîmatsâyanadugdhâbdhikaustubhena mahaujasâ |
kriyate mâdhavâryena sarvadarçanasangrahaḥ ||

and in the next verse that çrîmatsâyanamâdhavaḥ prabhuḥ composed it. Now if they were two persons the dual must have been used here.

4. There is a passage in some MSS. which runs:

sa (i. e. mâdhavaḥ) hy âha nrpatim, râjan! sâyanaryo mamâ 'nujaḥ |
sarvam vetty, esha vedânâm vyâkhyâtritve niyujyatâm ||
ity ukto mâdhavâryena vîrabukkamahîpatiḥ |
anvaçât sâyanâcâryam vedârthasya prakâçane ||

* "Rational Refutation" pp. 199 (n.) and 218 (n.) cfr. Çankara's C. on the Bhag. G. I.

ordinary honorific complement of S. Indian names. An equivalent name (but of Sanskrit origin) is Martu (i.e. martya). Sâyana's real name as a Brahman was, however, Mâdhavâcârya. If he had brothers, the name Sâyana shows that he must have been the eldest.

Vidyânagara favoured by an inaccessible position, and fortunate in energetic and competent rulers* soon assumed the position of the chief state in a confederation of the Hindu chiefs of the Deccan, and rapidly acquired influence over nearly the whole of Southern India. It is not therefore surprising that

---

This seems to render the above explanation impossible; it is however quite consistent. Mâdhava (the soul) as Brahma is eternal and Sâyana (the body) is therefore born subsequent (anuja) to it. The technical use of anuja for younger brother in the Law-books has caused the mistranslation of this passage and a very natural error on the part of Sanskritists. It must be remarked that Sâyana as a name precludes the existence of an *elder* brother by its peculiar application only to children whose elder brother or brethren have come to an untimely end. (See above p. x.)

5. In the later Vedic Commentaries Vidyâranyasvâmin is more consistent in his use of his other names than in his earlier ones. In the Yajurveda *Tândya* and *Rigveda* bhâshyas we find it said that king Bukka ordered Mâdhavâcârya to explain the Vedas, but all these works are stated in the colophons to have been composed by Sâyana. In the later commentaries we find that king Bukka ordered Sâyanâcârya to do so, and the colophon states that he is the author. It is very unlikely that this confusion which occurs only in MSS. of the Yajur *Tândya* and *Rigveda* bhâshyas can have arisen through copyist's errors.

The S. Indian tradition† is therefore correct, and the explanation of the facts is the one I have given above. The identification of Vidyâranyasvâmin with the guru of the Çringêri matha finally settles the question.

This strange allegory was probably used because ascetics are supposed to renounce all ceremonies and sacrifices.

*The Vidyânagara kingdom was always rather a confederation than the territory of one ruler, and even heretics were gladly welcomed. Thus the Ikkêri chief who was a Jain and (as inscriptions in the S. Canara province show) ruled above and below the ghats was one of the chief feudatories.

---

† As mentioned in my "Dâyavibhâga." (Madras 1868.) p. x. (n.).

the king should have provided for his minister's son by putting him in a fair way of becoming spiritual head of the very important sect to which his family belonged, the Smârttas a sect of Vedantists founded by Çankarâcârya. This sect has always cultivated the study of Sanskrit and especially of the Vedic literature, and though the earliest of the S. Indian orthodox sects, it has always held the highest reputation for learning and culture. The later sects have, each more than the others before it, neglected Vedic literature; the Vedantists have always made this the chief object of their studies, and there is not a work on the Vedic ritual composed in S. India by a person of another sect. The real commentaries on Vedic works not ostensibly written for sectarian purposes are also by Vedantists exclusively. For some centuries before the time of Sâyaṇa these studies had been pursued with some success. The Brahmans had had a hard fight with the Buddhists and Jains* and had barely got the victory and were thinking how to get over the compromises they had been obliged to make, when the Muhammadan invasion began. The Vedic system professed to explain all matters, and not only told what people should do, but also how it was possible to do almost anything; to conquer enemies or destroy them, to create wealth, to cure sickness and even to beat opponents in argument. For all these and countless other needs magical ceremonies or sacrifices are prescribed. It is thus intelligible how the subject attracted so much attention in the troubled times preceding and during Sâyaṇa's life. The head of the Smârttas is an ascetic (para-

*That the Nirgranthas (who according to the Chinese pilgrims Hiouen-Thsang formed the chief sect in S. India in the 7th century) were Jains, I have endeavoured to show in a note on p. 310 of vol. I., of the "Indian Antiquary."

mahamsaparivrâjakâcârya) of the strictest rule. The founder of the order, Çankarâcârya, seems to have in some respects imitated the Buddhists, in so far as he established mathas or monasteries for these ascetics, and released them from the life of wandering beggary which seems to have been exclusively the original rule.* The chief monastery or matha is that at Çringêri, a place near the sources of the Tungâ river and in the Mysore territory, but little to the east of the Western Ghats. At a considerable elevation above the sea level, Çringêri enjoys a comparatively fine climate. Twenty miles further to the west is the damp hot coast of Canara and the Konkan, where energy must not be looked for. Mysore is however dry and rocky, and its people are far more energetic in mind and body than those of the low country. To Europeans however, and occasionally to natives, the climate is none of the best, as it is peculiarly subject to epidemics of malarious fever; but to the last (who are practically fatalists) this seems no serious objection, and so important is the effect of belief, that the series of the âcâryas of Çringêri shows as a rule exceptionally long lives. An abstemious and celibate life is still observed by the âcâryas, but the accompanying portrait of the worthy actual âcârya will show how far the old

* The original Brahman rule is to be found in some of the Upanishads, especially the Kaivalya (to be printed in my "*Index to the Tanjore MSS.*") Arunika and Jâbâla Upanishads; and is corroborated by the Greek accounts (Megasthenes, ed. Schwanbeck, p. 12:). Both it and the Nirgrantha rule did not contemplate a fixed residence at any place even for a short while; the Buddhist rule however allowed the monks to live in convents during the rainy season (varshâ cfr. *Burnouf's "Introduction"* p. 285); and the Hindu ascetics of the orthodox sects resemble them in that they must reside for their câturmâsya, as it is called, in a convent, but *may* wander the rest of the year. The Buddhist Varshâvasana was also for four months.

rule is neglected, and how much these Indian ascetics resemble the Tibetan Lamas. There is only one âcârya or guru, at a time, and the rule is, that he, when in expectation of death, should select a pupil who is a Brahmacârin (or celibate) to succeed him in the order (âçrama), and this is done by communicating to him the secret mantra of the office (upadeça.)* According to the list of these pontiffs† preserved at Çringêri, Mâdhavâcârya became Jagadguru in succession to çrî Bhâratîtîrtha‡ on the 7th day of the bright fortnight (çukla) in the month of Kârttika (November) of the year called Prajotpatti, 1253 of the Çâlivâhana era (=1331 A. D.). Popular tradition makes him to have been then thirty-six years of age, an estimate in every way probable.

In the safe retirement of Çringêri he had ample time to compose his voluminous Commentaries; his position was as favorable for this purpose as it is possible to imagine, and he must have had ample means. The matha has always possessed considerable landed property, and the monopoly of the sandalwood grown on it, alone, must have always furnished a considerable revenue. In addition to this, it is the duty of all the Vedantists (in Southern India at least) to send con-

---

* This rule of succession renders possible an accurate chronology of much of the later Sanskrit literature, as I indicated in a letter in the "Academy" iii., p. 419. That there should be only one guru at a time in a matha follows from his semi-divine character; matha means properly a temple, as Amarâcârya says: "devâlayo devagriham caityam âyatanam mathah |" (Nâmamâlâ).

† A list of the succession of the gurus must be kept at every matha in order to perform their commemorations. In this respect as in many others, these mathas bear a most striking resemblance to the great religious houses of the same period in Europe. The Çringeri list (but without dates) has long been printed. v. Wilson's Works by Rost. i. p. 201 n.

‡ In the preface to this "Parâçarasmritivyâkhyâ" Mâdhava pays reverence to him as his guru.

ಶ್ರೀ ಶೃಂಗೇರಿ ನೃಸಿಂಹ ಭಾರತಿ
ಸ್ವಾಮಿಗಳವರ ಭಾವ ಚಿತ್ರ ॥೦॥

tributions according to a fixed scale to the guru, and which are collected by agents and farmers; produce in large quantities is also sent by devout followers. His life was also an unusually long one for a native of India, for he was Jagadguru for 55 years and died (never to be born again) in the year Xaya, 1308 of the era of Çâlivâhana (=1386 A. D.) probably ninety-one years of age, and certainly not less than eighty.*

His works tell us nearly all that is important in the history of the rest of his recluse life—the order in which they were brought out. Their exact dates are not known, and it is little likely that they ever will be,† but the chief period of his literary activity seems to range between 1350 and 1380 A. D.; the beginning and end of Bukka's reign at Vidyânagara. The dates of the kings of that town are uncertain to a greater or lesser degree, as they depend entirely upon mention in inscriptions.‡

We also know that he had at least one pupil, Râmakrishna, who commented on his master's Pañcadaçasî, probably his last book.

---

* The exact date given by the obituary list mentioned above is: "Monday the 13th of Jeshtha çukla of Xaya çâlivâhanaçakâbda 1308" i. e. toward the end of May. An inscription of Çak. 1318 (=1391) speaks of him as already dead. (Bombay A. S. J. iv. 115. and ix. 227.)

† No known autograph exists even at Çringêri, and there can be no other means of ascertaining the exact dates.

‡ Of the two chronologies upon this basis which differ at the most by half a dozen years in the beginnings of the several reigns, the oldest is that in As. Res. xx. which has been followed by Lassen (I. A. K. iv. Appendix) though (as usual) he gives a number of imperfect and therefore—in the presence of the inscriptions—worthless traditions. The last is by Mr. C. P. Brown in his "Cyclic Tables" (Madras 1850) which is based upon the examination of a much larger number of inscriptions and therefore more trustworthy. The genealogy of the family is far more certain; inscriptions of the time of each king exist in abundance, and we have also accounts which are nearly contemporaneous. The most important of these is Caundappa's preface to his

Sâyana's first work was the [1]Vedântâdhikarana-ratnamâlâ a compendium of all the topics of the Vedânta system in verse, and explained in prose*. He then took up the Dharmaçâstra and wrote a Commentary on the smriti attributed to Parâçara, which he called [2]Parâçarasmri-

---

[*Apastamba*] Prayogaratnamâlâ in which he gives an account of the dynasty of Vidyânagara, and as he was *mantrin* to Çrîvîrabhûpati his information cannot be questioned. His account of the family which is corroborated by inscriptions gives the following genealogy:

Sangama (of the Yâdava family of the Lunar race))

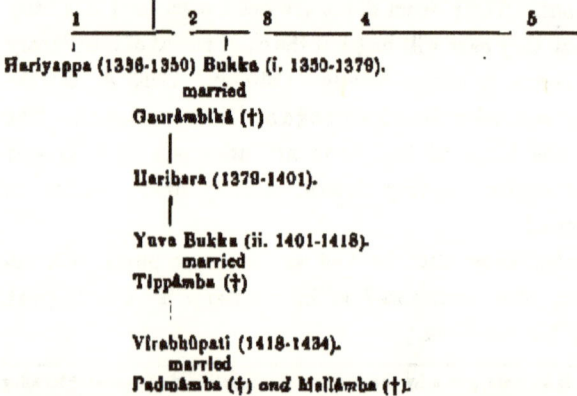

1 | 2 | 3 | 4 | 5

Hariyappa (1336-1350) Bukka (i. 1350-1379).

married

Gaurâmbikâ (†)

Harihara (1379-1401).

Yuva Bukka (ii. 1401-1418).

married

Tippâmba (†)

Vîrabhûpati (1418-1434).

married

Padmâmba (†) *and* Mallâmba (†).

We have an excellent account of Vidyânagara by Abd er-Razzak who was there in 1442, which is corroborated by European travellers of about the same time, Conti and Nikitin. The last describes its capture by the Muhammadans about the end of the century. The ruins still remain, and are in a tolerably fair state of preservation; the temples are occasionally the scene of pilgrimages. Modern maps mark the site mostly by the name Hampe; it is in the Bellary District of the Madras Presidency.

*It begins: Pranamya paramâtmânam çrîvidyâtîrtharûpinam |
Vaiyyâsikanyâyamâlâ çlokaih sangrihyate sphutam ||
prârîpsitasya granthasya nirvighnena parisamâptipracayagamanâya çistâcâra-paripâlanâya ca viçisteshtadevatâtatvam gurumûrtyupâdhiyuktam namaskritya grantham pratijânite, etc.

---

† These names have all originally the Dravidian complement of female names—amma, (i. e. mother), but have been Sanskritized to suit the verse.

tivyâkhyâ. He did this, as he says, because it had not been annotated by any one previously,* but he was not very successful. His Commentary is an immense mass of quotations which obscure rather than explain the text, and the best part of it is the third kâṇḍa (Vyavahâramâdhava on Jurisprudence) intended to supply the omission of the text which treats only of âçâra and prâyaçcitta, but it is nearly all abridged from the mitâxarâ and similar older law-books.† The 3) Kâlamâdhava is a sort of supplement to the whole, and treats of the astrological determination of times for ceremonies, and of the calendar. He then treated the Pûrvamîmâṃsâ system on the same plan as he had done the Uttaramîmâṃsâ (Vedânta) in his first work. His treatise, the 4) Jaiminîyanyâyamâlâvistara, is well known by the late Dr. Goldstücker's nearly complete edition.

All these works appear to have been written after Bukka's accession about 1350‡; the first does not mention any patron, but the second and fourth allude to that sovereign in terms which almost amount to a dedication. That in the middle of the 14th century these works attracted much attention is natural, and they were, no doubt, the cause why this devout§ king selected their author to annotate and explain the Vedas. That the plan originated with the king, Sâyaṇa himself states; it was part of his attempt to restore Hinduism, and must always remain their best joint title to remembrance,

*See çloka 9 of the preface.

†The first two kâṇḍas have been printed (not edited) at Madras in the Telugu character, 874 pp. 4°. 1871. Of the third kâṇḍa, I printed a translation of the part on inheritance: "Dâyavibhâga" Rl. 8vo. pp. XV., 67 and II. Madras, 1868.

‡The fourth mentions the first and second as already finished, and the Vedic Commentaries all mention the first and fourth as written before them.

§Vaidikamârgapravartaka and Vedabhâshyapravartaka are the usual epithets applied to Bukka and Harihara in inscriptions of the time.

for, considering the perpetual troubles extending all over India in the 14th century the scheme was a magnificent one, and **Sâyana** nearly completed it. That **Bukka** originated it, is stated by **Sâyana** in the introductory verses prefixed to all these commentaries, but as **Harihara** assumes also the title of **Vedabhâshyapravartaka** it is most likely that what we have were written in both **Bukka's** and **Harihara's** reigns, or from about 1350 to 1386 in which year **Sâyana** died. All the commentaries on the Vedic **Samhitâs** and **Brâhmanas** were to form parts of one immense work, the **Mâdhavîyavedârthaprakâça**, and the first place is given to the [5)] **Taittirîyasamhitâ** on account of its importance for sacrificial purposes.* The [6)] **Taittirîyabrâhmana** and [7)] ***Aranyaka***† come next, and then follows his greatest work the [8)] ***Rigvedabhâshya***‡. He next commented on the [9)] **Aitareyabrâhmana**§ at considerable length, and then, but more briefly, the [10)] **Aitareyâranyaka**||, and

---

* *Rigveda bh.* p. 1. "Adhvaryavasya yajneshu prâdhânyâd vyâkritah purâ Yajurvedo" etc.

† Taitt. *Ar.*, pp. 1 & 2

"Vyâkhyâtâ . . . . taittirîyakasamhitâ | tadbrâhmanam ça vyâkhyâtam, çishtam âranyakam tatah" ||

‡ *R. V.* p. 1. "vyâkritah purâ yajurvedo 'tha hautrârtham *rigvedo* vyâkarishyate" ||

§ The only MSS. I know of is at Tanjore (No. 2,379) and it does not mention the order in which it was written, as the preface contains only the first four çlokas which occur in all these Commentaries.

|| Of this work also I have seen only one MS. which forms part of No. 1, of the *Whish* collection in the library of the Royal Asiatic Society of London. It is in the *Malayâlam* character and begins on p. 152, b. but is very incorrect and imperfect. After the usual first four *çlokas*, Sâyana continues:

"aitareyabrâhmane trikândam âranyakâbhidham |
aranya eva pâthyam syâd âranyakamitârthakam ||
âranyakâni pânca 'ti proktâny arthavibhedatah |
mahâvratam ahah proktam prathamâranyake sphutam ||

Sattraprakarane" etc.

next turned his attention to the Sâmaveda. Of this he explained the [11]Samhitâ* and the eight Brâhmanas: [12]Tândya, [13]Shadvimça, [14]Sâmavidhâna, [15]Arsheya, [16]Devatâdhyâya, [17]Upanishad†, [18]Samhitopanishad, and [19]Vamça.‡

Sâyana also wrote a number of Commentaries and treatises of the dates of which I cannot find any information either because I have not been able to inspect MSS. or because accessible information is imperfect. Some of these relate to the Vedas, and the most important is his Commentary on the [20]Çatapatha-Brâhmana of the white Yajurveda. Extracts from this have been printed in Dr. Weber's edition of the text. He is also reported to have commented on his own ritual the [21]Baudhâyanasûtra, but I have never seen a copy of this work. His general treatise on the Vedic ritual, [22]Yajnatantrasudhânidhi exists, and I have seen at Tanjore a fragment.§ Those remaining to be mentioned are of a miscellaneous character. The [23]Dhâtuvritti is one of the most important; it is an elaborate commentary on the Sanskrit roots recognized by the followers of the grammatical

---

*Sâmavedabhâshya, pref. çl. 10-11.

. . . . yajuh |
vyâkhyâtam prathamam paççâd ricâm vyâkhyânam îritam ||
sâmnâm rigâçritatvena sâmavyâkhyâ 'tha varnyate |
anushthânânujijnânâvaçâd vyâkhyâkramo hy ayam ||

†Profr. Max Müller adopts Weber's suggestion ("Ancient Sanskrit Lit." p. 349) that a Commentary on the Chândogya brâhmana is here intended. This is probably correct. Sâyana's C. on the Mantraparva of the Sâmabrâhmana appears to be on the first two Chapters of the Chândogya brâhmana (see my Catalogue pp. 52, 3.) Besides the MS. which I have described there is another in the Government Library at Madras in the nandinâgarî character, but much injured.

‡This order is mentioned in the C. on the Vamçabrâhm. See çlokas 5—8.

§No. 4,150.

School of Pâṇini, and was written before his Vedic Commentaries, as he quotes it in them. The [24]Sarvadarçanasaṅgraha is a very fair statement of the doctrines of the chief heterodox philosophico-religious schools of thought current in India in the 14th century. With the exception of a commentary on the [25]Mânavadharmaçâstra which I have not seen, but believe to be still in existence, Sâyṇa's remaining works relate to the doctrine of the important sect of which he was so long the chief pontiff. The [26]Sarvopanishadarthânubhûtiprakâça is a paraphrase in verse of the twelve chief Upanishads;* the [27]Çaṅkaravijaya is a sort of historical romance based on the life of the founder of South Indian Vedantism—Çaṅkarâcârya,† and the [28]Jîvanmuktiviveka, a treatise on the spiritual state he had himself reached, and in which a perfect apprehension of ones own identity with Brahma brings about identity of subject and object or union with that only truly existing Being, though the corporeal part yet remains to exhaust its power of fruition.

Probably Vidyâraṇyasvâmin's last work was the [29]Pañcadaçî, an account of the Vedânta system in a popular and easy style. At the end we find

priyâd dhariharo 'nena brahmânandena sarvadâ |
pâyâc ca prâṇinaḥ sarvân svâçritân chuddhamanasân ||

It must therefore have been written after 1379, about which

---

*Profr. Cowell has edited an extract from it in his edition of the Kaushîtakî Up. See also *Hall's* "Contributions" etc. p. 116.

†It seems very doubtful if this is really a work of Sâyaṇa, as Dr. Hall ("Contributions" p. 167) states, that in the MSS. he examined the author, Mâdhava, calls himself Abhinavakâlidâsa. Aufrecht ("Catalogus" p. 252) does not mention this. In S. India the Çaṅkaravijaya is attributed to Vidyâraṇyasvâmin or Sâyaṇa, but it certainly is not worthy of him. The author was evidently a native of Southern India.

year the reign of Harihara seems to have begun. It is a well known work and much read even to the present day. A loose paraphrase exists in Tamil, and forms a favorite text-book.*

Some time ago, Dr. Haug published a statement made to him by the Gujarat Brâhmans that Sâyana had also left a Commentary on the Samhitâ and Brâhmana of the Atharvaveda†, but there is every reason to believe that he was mis-informed. There is no trace of it to be found at present, as far as I am aware, and though Sâyana evidently had seen the samhitâ‡ of this Veda it seems exceedingly doubtful if he would have written a book for which he could have had no readers in his own country, and Southern India; for there is no doubt whatever that the Atharvaveda is entirely foreign to all the Madras Presidency or country of the Dravidian languages. There are, it is true, a few MSS. in the Palace Library at Tanjore, but they were brought there from Benares within the last 50 years; I am informed also that two or three families of Atharvaveda Brahmans are quite recently settled at Mysore. The best informed Pandits in S. India however, persistently deny the existence at all of this Veda, and utterly disbelieve in the book published by Roth and Whitney! As Sâyana neglected to comment on Vedic works like the Kaushî-

---

* *Dr. Graul* has translated this into German in the first vol. of his "Bibliotheca Tamulica." 1854, pp. 98—172.

† Z. d. d. m. G. xviii., p. 804 (where he mentions it as existing in the Madras Presidency), and again p. 838 where he says: "Sâyana's Commentar zur Samhitâ and Brahmana des Atharva ist in Ahmedabad; ich hoffe eine abschrift des seltenen Buchs zu erhalten."

‡ *Rig V. Bhâshya*, i. p. 2. "Âtharvanikair api svakîyasamhitâyâm ṛica eva bâhulyenâ 'dhîyante." He again quotes the Âtharvanikâh in his Yajurvedabhâshya, i. p. 7.

takibrâhmana, copies of which he could have had in Malabar, it seems improbable that he would have sought out a book not recognized in S. India.*

Vidyâranyasvâmin's literary activity thus extended over about thirty years or from 1350—1380. He had ample time to compose his numerous works which are nothing like so extensive as those of some of the schoolmen, and there are thus no real grounds for supposing, as has repeatedly been done† that he was in the habit of lending his name to works composed by others. This has been as often done in India as elsewhere, but Vidyâranyasvâmin's position almost precludes the possibility of its having occurred in his case, and the inconsistency of his interpretations is fully explained by the nature of his works. Authority is paramount in India; not

---

*Dr. Haug, ("Brahma und die Brahmanen" p. 45) quotes the introduction to Patanjali's Mahâbhâshya as a proof of the antiquity of the A. V.; the S. Indian MSS. however omit the quotation from the A. V.

†Perhaps to add a fictitious value to his Commentaries. H. H. Wilson (*Rigveda Samhita* vol. I., p. xlix.) says "The fact, no doubt, being, that they ("the two brothers") availed themselves of those means which their situation and influence secured them, and employed the most learned Brahmans they could attract to Vijayanagara upon the works which bear their name, and to which they also contributed their labour and learning. Their works were, therefore, compiled under peculiar advantages, and are deservedly held in the highest estimation." Lassen (I. A. K. iv., pp. 172-3) "Mâdhavâkârja und sein Bruder Sâjanâkârja haben eine bedeutende Anzahl von Werken dieser Art hinterlassen; von einigen derselben muss es vorläufig noch dahingestellt bleiben, ob sie nicht dem ersteren aus Schmeichelei zugeschrieben worden seien." Also Roth (in Z. d. d. M. G. xxi., pp. 3. 4.) considers that assistance was given, but differs from Wilson in his estimate of its value. The Vidyânagara dynasty was certainly very liberal to Brahmans, but (though I have looked through many of the still existing grants) I have not as yet seen a single case in which a grant was beyond doubt made to a N. Indian Brahman. Thus there is no reason for supposing that foreign "learned Brahmans" were attracted there.

necessarily the authority of predecessors, but that of the Guru who is regarded as infallible. V i d y â r a n y a s v â m i n being "g u r u of the world" to whom could he submit his judgment? Indeed of such influences there are naturally no traces apparent in his existing works, but circumstances rendered it impossible for him to be a consistent critic. In the first place the Vedânta system is a flat contradiction to the old vedic religion, and for V i d y â r a n y a s v â m i n to comment on the Vedic s a m h i t â s is much the same as if a Christian priest at Rome in the present day taught, bonâ fide, augury and the method of sacrificing to Jupiter and the other old heathen gods. So illogical a state of mind must produce illogical results. Again his method was defective, and his views those of a systematizer who seeks to reduce all into conformity with his pre-conceived notions. The logic of the m î m â m s â is excellent, but it is tainted by the natural results of the principle that the Vedic texts in reality constitute a whole that is in every respect in harmony with itself. Nor does the Vedânta system profess more than to tolerate the sacrifices as a method of procuring temporal benefits, but the great and final end is m o x a or deliverance from separate and sensual existance. It is then impossible to suppose that S â y a n a took up the matter from an indifferent critical stand-point; he was an orthodox Hindu pontiff of a particular sect, and wrote his commentary from that point of view; he was a great theologian of his day and sect, but not a critic. The S â n k h y a-v e d â n t a School of Ç a n k a r â c â r y a, which was at once his religion and philosophical system, was in many ways opposed to the m î m â m s â system he also used, and that he used both is not only evident from his works,* but he even states that he had written on these two subjects before commenting on the Vedas, as an additional reason in recommendation of his own commentaries.† Sectarian commentaries on Vedic works appear to have begun with Gaudapâda, Çankara and their followers, and were confined at first to the Upanishads, (at least, Çankara and Râmânuja appear to have gone no farther); but a little more than a century before Sâyana and at a distance of only two days' journey from his convent, Anandatîrtha (Madhvâcârya) had founded a sect to which Sâyana seems to have had a great dislike‡ and with which he was evidently well acquainted, and one of the chief works which this sect follows is a Rigbhâshya by this same Anandatîrtha. Sâyana was however by no means without predecessors of his own sect (with perhaps one exception, as will be shown

---

*It is clearly by an oversight that Profr. Goldstücker asserted the contrary ("Pânini's Place" separate edition, p. 248): "all his (Sâyana's) explanations show that he stands on the ground of the *oldest legends and traditions*, of such traditions, moreover, as have no connection whatever with the creed of those sects which represent the degenerated Hindu faith in his time."

H. H. Wilson considered Sâyana "a competent" but not "infallible interpreter" ("Rigvedasamhitâ" II., p. xxix) in which opinion Dr. Goldstücker appears later to have agreed; even Lassen (I. A. K. iv. p. 178) had already noticed as Vidyâranya's prominent weakness, that he attributed to words of the text later philosophical meanings; in what way however Lassen did not point out). This process is one which all sacred records invariably undergo, and Dr. Brugsch has remarked it of the ancient Egyptian texts. ("Die sage von der geflügelten sonnenscheibe," 1870 pp. 4. & 5.)

† Ye pûrvottaramîmâmse te vyâkhyâyâ 'tisangrahât |
kripâluh sâyanâcâryo vedârtham vaktum udyatah ‖

In one inscription at least (Bombay As. Soc. J. iv., p. 115 and ix., p. 227) Mâdhava (or Vidyâranya) is spoken of as Upanishanmârgapravartaka, an epithet which clearly shows that his contemporaries thought him a religious leader and a champion of a doctrine little known before.

‡ Sarvadarçanasangraha, p. 61, where he talks of his "pretence" to comment on the Brahmamîmâmsâ. Madhvâcârya was born in 1121, died in 1197.

below) who had written Commentaries on some of the Vedic samhitâs. The founders of brahmanical sects in S. India, based their doctrine ultimately on the Vedas, and their Commentaries written in a party-spirit were the means by which they succeeded; it was thus impossible that Vidyâranya could escape such influences. So much for the state of mind with which he approached his work, and the only "traditional" interpretation or rather method that he can be said to have possessed.

He had also the relics of the old etymological school of interpretation such as Yâska has preserved, and which seems to have been the only real and bonâ fide school of vedic interpretation that ever existed in India, and he made great use of not only Yâska but also of Pânini, whose works he doubtless knew by heart, as also one vedic samhitâ at least*. Of the old legends which are often quoted to explain Vedic passages he also had a good store, but that these rest on mere misunderstandings and vain conjectures has been conclusively shown by Dr. Max Müller.† Less than this he could hardly have been provided with, considering that, he as a pupil of his predecessor must have undergone a long novitiate devoted to these studies. But, as has often been pointed out, Sâyana falters in his etymologies, and even contradicts himself; I think it may be also added that he even forces the grammatical sûtras to

* Vidyâranya's father is styled dvivedin or professor of two Vedas (Yajur and *Rig*veda probably) in an inscription mentioned in the Bombay As. Soc. J. ix., p. 226. Dr. Bhau Dâji however doubts the authenticity of this document, because Caundibhatta is mentioned in it as Mâdhava's father and Mâcâmba as his mother.

† "Hymns of the Gaupâyanas and the legend of king Asamâti" (in Journal of the R. As. Soc. of London, N. S. II., pp. 426—479), a paper which marks a notable epoch in Vedic studies.

countenance his own interpretations. As a theologian he was bound to do so. His Mîmâmsâ and Vedânta systems told him that the Veda was perfectly free from inconsistency, and he therefore was justified in doing what he did. He could not look critically on passages as Europeans do now-a-days.

The chief source from whence he compiled consisted, however, in the labours of predecessors in the same field.* Some of these he mentions; and nearly all can be still consulted in S. Indian MSS., and the result of even a superficial comparison is that Vidyâranya used these older commentaries to an extent little suspected. Of the works he consulted for his great Rigvedabhâshya, there is unfortunately but little information; the Commentary by Skandasvâmin has not yet been discovered, and this is the one mentioned by Vidyâranya in that work. But Prof. Max Müller considers that Atmânanda's Commentary, is also anterior to it, though not quoted.† Dr. Hall has brought to light a Râvanabhâshya‡ also believed to be earlier than Vidyâranya's, according to Dr. Haug, and this same scholar has also ascertained the existence of another old commentary, the Kauçikabhâshya.§ Besides these I found at Tanjore fragments of a commentary on the Rigveda called Gûdhârtharatnamâlâ which appears to be older than, or at all events independent of Vidyâranya's Commentary, and which mentions a previous work of the same kind, hitherto unknown.|| It

* Haug "Ait. Brâhmana" I., preface, p. vi. Max Müller A. S. L. p. 240 (n.)
† A. S. L. do.

‡ Journal Bengal As. Soc. xxxi. See also his "Contributions" p. 119.
§ Ait. Br. i., pref. vi.

|| This fragment (No. 6,979 of the Palace Library) is on a few much broken palm leaves and the author's name is not given. On the first leaf is: bhagavatparatvaprakâçapradarçanârtham sajjanânujighrixur bhagavân ânarthamunih

would be idle (in the absence of their works) to speculate as to what schools Skandasvâmin* and the author of the Kauçikabhâshya belonged. The name *Â*tmânanda leaves no doubt as to his having been a Vedantist; the Râva*n*abhâshya must have been of the same school, as it is quoted to support Vedantic doctrine. The Gû*d*hârtharatnamâlâ states that, according to the *R*igveda, Nârâya*n*a is the Supreme Being, and it is therefore also Vedantist. Respecting the Yajurvedabhâshya there is more satisfactory information, for Bha*tt*a Bhâskara's Commentary which Vidyâra*n*ya quotes is still in existence.† It is difficult to say to what sect he belonged, but he seems to have been one of the old school of Vedantists that worshipped Çiva as the Supreme Being. He alludes to earlier Commentaries by Bhavasvâmin and others which "treated only of the meaning of words;" his own work is therefore perhaps the first systematic Commentary on any of the Vedas. There are evidences on every page‡ that Sâya*n*a merely worked again over Bha*tt*a Bhâskara's book, and introduced a number of mîmâ*m*sist and similar discussions which certainly have not improved it. In fact he has been almost servile in his copying in some parts. As Dr. A. Weber pointed out long ago (Indische Studien i. p. 76), Sâya*n*a mentions in his Commentary on the Taittirîyâra*n*yaka, that several recensions existed

(? âoarttamanlâ) kâsâmold vicâm bhâshyam acîklripat: tadbhâshyam apy atigahanârthatvân madais sukhena jnâtum na çakyata iti para.........(broken off). This old commentary was therefore written with a sectarian object also.

* All that is known of Skandasvâmin is to be found in Devarâja's preface to his Nighantubhâshya printed below on pp. xxi. flg. His etymologies quoted in the same work are mostly very uncertain, and no better than those of the other commentators.

† See my "Catalogue of a Collection of Sanskrit MSS." p. 12 flg.

‡ See especially his preface and Vidyâranya's to their respective Commentaries on the Taitt. *Â*ranyaka. ("Catalogue," pp. 16, 17.)

of part of this appendix to the Black Yajurveda; the Dravidians had 64 sections in their 10th prapâthaka, the Ândhras 60 and so on.* Sâyana adopts the Ândhra recension which was that commented on by Bhatta Bhâskara and is current in N. India, but he omits to mention that the S. Indian recensions differ also materially in the earlier prapâthakas, and that in these he copies servilely the earlier Commentator, who followed a recension all but unknown in the South. There the sections of the Taittirîyâranyaka are called praçna, and of these the first three agree with the first three prapâthakas of Sâyana's text; the fourth with his sixth; the fifth with his seventh, eighth and ninth; the sixth with his tenth; and the seventh and eighth with his fourth and fifth; *generally*, but not in particulars, for the introductory benedictions are generally omitted, and the division into sections is different. He must have been well aware of this important fact yet he passes it over in silence.

If we look at the Sâmavedabhâshya, it is plain that Sâyana has simply copied Bharatasvâmin's Commentary written about the end of the 13th or beginning of the 14th century in Mysore, and by a Vedantist, as his name shows.† Bharatasvâmin, like all the older commentators, is very wild in his etymologies, and gives a number of guesses at each hard, or even easy, word. Of these Sâyana makes a selection and takes, certainly, the best.

So far, then, Sâyana had a written tradition to guide him; he seems to have been the earliest commentator on the other Vedic works mentioned above, and here, where he was

*p. 753 of the Bibl. Indica edition (by Rajendralâl Mitra).

†Catalogue. pp. 39, 40.

left to himself,* it is easy to see how little the etymological treatises on which he relied, could aid him. He applies the grammatical sûtras in a mechanical way, and never quotes parallel passages. Nor are his predecessors superior to him in this respect. His Commentaries on the smaller Brâhmaṇas of the Sâmaveda, show what his independent work is, and none better than the one now printed.

As far as oral tradition is concerned there is little reason to suppose that he got much help thus. With all the labours of the grammarians the pronunciation of Sanskrit differs in many parts of India. In Malabar, for example, tasmât and tatsama are written തസ്മാൽ and തൽസമ tasmâl and talsama, and pronounced accordingly†; and so also wherever ṭ or t comes before another consonant. The true pronunciation of the Vedic accents is admittedly lost, and at the present day a Nambûri (or Malabar Brahman) recites the Vedic texts in a way that is unintelligible to a Tamil Brahman. Nor are the details of the sacrifices better known; two distinct plants are used for the soma by the Tamil and Malabar Brahmans. Nor do the Indian commentators refer to oral tradition; in their prefaces they mention occasionally the "practice of the good" or "learned" as an authority, and very rarely perhaps quote

---

*A striking instance of this occurs in his Sâmavedabhâshya. For the Pûrvârcika, he had Bharatasvâmin before him, but this commentator did not go any further, and accordingly we see Vidyâraṇya's C. on the Uttarârcika assume a totally different character, so that as Benfey ("Sâmaveda" p. xl. cfr. also p. xxi.) justly remarks, the CC. on the Pûrva and Uttara ârcikas can hardly be taken as by the same hand. Probably the similar condition of the later parts of his Ṛigvedabhâshya is owing to the same cause; viz., that help failed him there.

†Bartholomæus a Sancto Paulino wrote thus in his "Vyacaranam" and was then most undeservedly attacked by the Calcutta students of Sanskrit. He was wrong in many matters, but right in this!

a custom, but no more. It is evident that such a source of information must have been a cause of weakness rather than of strength, and, that it was *always** admitted in India is a fact as much against a theory that traditions have been preserved unimpaired in that country from the earliest times, as is the admitted existence of an enormous number of çâkhâs, or schools, not only advocating different recensions of the same text, but which also supported a difference in the ritual. A *growth* in many ways must have occurred, and that up to recent times.

That the above view of the information possessed by the Indian Commentators is the only possible one, is also shown by their own account of their way of setting to work. The two following passages are the most explicit I know of the kind the first is from the introduction to Cau*n*d*a*ppâcârya's *A*pastambaprayogaratnamâlâ, written at Vidyânagara within fifty years after Sâya*n*a's death; it mentions exactly all the resources at his command, and as he was like Sâya*n*a, in high office (a mantrin or minister), it can only be supposed that he had every possible advantage. I take this extract from Tanjore MS. No. 3,854:—

sa kadâcid bhûpatîndra*h*† pâlayan dharmata*h* prajâ*h* |
sa*m*prârthito dvijai*h* çrauta*m* viçadîkartum udyata*h* || 19 ||
vicârya vidushâ*m* madhye Cau*nd*appâryam adidiçat |
vyâcaxvâ 'dhvaratantra*m* tva*m* samantrârtham iti sphu*t*a*m* || 20 ||
. . . .
utsâhî sarvak*r*ityeshu prabhumantry anujadvaya*h* |
Cau*nd*appâryo 'martyavarya*h* (? 'mâtyavarya*h*) so 'bhûd bhûpatibhûpate*h* || 25 ||

*Cfr. the Brâhmanas passim. *A*pastambadharmasûtra, I., 1, 1. Baudhâyana do: (in my "Catalogue," p. 34). Mânavadharmaçâstra. xii., 108.

† Vîrabhûpati, son of Bukka II., and who reigned from 1418—1434.

sadgurûpâttasadvidyo Vishnubhattâryasûktibhiḥ |
vidvatprayogam sakalam kratûnâm âkaromy aham || 26 ||
kalpasûtreshv anekeshu sarvakratusamanvayât |
Âpastambâcâryasûtram pradhânam pracaratvataḥ || 27 ||
vyâkhyâsyate ca tatsûtram hautraudgâtr[a]prasangataḥ |
sûtrârthamantravâkyârthaprayogapratipâdanaiḥ || 28 ||
brâhmanam kalpasûtrâni mîmâmsânyâyavistarau |
tarkavyâkarano chando niruktajyotishî api || 29 ||
vedabhâshyâni sarvâni smrti[m] tatsangrahân api |
sûtravyâkhyâs tathâ sarvâ âcâram tadvidâm api|| 30 ||
kalâvidyâçilpavidy[e] api samçodhya yatnataḥ |
prayogaratnamâlo 'yam tanyate hridayangamâ || 31 ||

It is obvious that there is nothing mentioned here which cannot be referred to at the present day, except perhaps that the priests now are probably more careless and ignorant than those Caundappa could consult, and much fewer in number.

The next extract (also from a Tanjore MS. No. 2,385) is Devarâja's preface to his Nighantubhâshya. He was, as appears below, a native of the South of India, and the Rangeçapurî in a suburb of which he tells us that he resided is probably Seringapatam;* as he mentions Mâdhava (i.e. Vidyâranya-Sâyana) he cannot be earlier than the 15th though he is probably not later than the 16th century.

Bhagavatâ yâskena samâmnâyam naighantukanaigamadevatâkândarûpena vividham gavâdidevapatnyantam nirbruvatâ naigamadevatâkândapathitâni padâni pratyekam upâdâya niruktâni darçitâni nigamâni ca, naighantukândaparipathitânâm tu gavâdyapâre-antânâm ekacatvârimçacchatatrayâdhikam sa-

*The other one is Sîrîngam (Çrîranga) close to Trichinopoly.

haeram sâmânyena "etâvanty asya sattvasya nâmadheyânî" 'ti vyâkhyâya tatra pradarçya katicid eva niruktâni tathâ 'pi kânicid eva darçitâni nigamâni, anyâni tu granthavistarabhîtyâ sâmânye nirvacanalaxanasyo 'ktatvâd buddhimadbhir nirvaktum suçakânî 'ty abhiprâyena co 'pexitâni. Skandasvâmî ca tata eva niruktam anujagâma. Tatra tu divaç câ 'dityasya ca sâdhârananâmâni svarâdîni shat; idamâdîni ca upamâbhedâd bhedanâmâni dvâdaça; prapitve abhîke ityâdîni shadvimçatiç ca bhâshyakârena bahuvaktavyatvât prakarana eva niruktâni Skandasvâminâ ca vyâkhyâtâni. Ato 'nyeshâm yathâkramenâ 'nirukter nigamâpradarçanâc ca svarûpamâtram apy adhyayanâd evâ 'vagantavyam. Tac câ 'dhyayanam kaliyuge prâyena vicchinnasampradâyam âsît. Teshu ca keshucid artheshu lekhakapramâdâdibhih kânicit padâny adhikâny âsan anyeshu ca kânicin nyûnâni. Apareshu ca kânicid apahâya kânicit visrastâni, axarâni ca viparyastâni. Evam vyûkîrneshu koçeshu niyamaikabhûtasya pratipadanirvacananigamapradarçanaparasya kasyacid vyâkhyânasyâ 'bhâvân naighantukam kândam utsannaprâyam âsît. Tataç ca pâthasamçodhanârtham bâlânâm sugamatvâya ca tadgatânâm kramena pratipadam nirvacananigamau pradarçayitum svarâdînî 'ti pûrvam uktasya prakaranatrayasya naigame devatâkândagatânâm ca padânâm ca bhâshyakârena niruktânâm Skandasvâminâ kritavyâkhyânânâm prakriyâyâm unmîlayitavyam. Bahu vastu ca naighantukakândanirvacanânantaram, tad unmîlayitum câ 'yam asmat pariçramah. Idam ca svamanîshikayâ na kriyate, kimtu naighant[uk]agateshv eva padeshv adhyardhaçatatrayamâtrâni padâni bhâshyakârenai 'va tatra nigameshu prasangân niruktâni; Skandasvâminâ ca nigamavyâkhyâneshv anyâni ca padâni çatadvayamâtrâny upâttâni. Tena ca samâmnâyapathitânâm padânâm anyebhyo vyâvrityartham kimcic cihnam na kritam. Atas teshâm pâthaçuddhis tatrai 'va çuddhâ. Anyeshâm ca pad(ân)âm asmatkule samâmnâyâdhyayanasya(? â) vicchedât, çrî Venkatâcâryatanayasya Mâdhavasya bhâshyakrit(o) nâmânukramanyâ âkhyânânukramanyâ nipâtânukramanyâ nirvacanânukramanyâ(s), tadîyasya bhâshyasya ca bahuçah paryâlocanâd bahudeçasamânîtabahukoçanirîxanâc ca pâthah samçodhitah, nirvacanam ca niruktam. Skandasvâmikritâm niruktatîkâm, Skandasvâmi-bhavasvâmi-guhadeva-çrînivâsa-mâdhavadeva-ûvata-bhattabhâskaramiçra-bharatasvâmyâdiviracitâni vedabhâshyâni pâninîyam vyâkaranam viçeshata unâditadvrittixîrasvâmy-anantâcâryâdikritanighantuvyâkhyâ bhojârâjîyam vyâkaranam kamalanayanîyanikhilapadarâjiç ca nirîxya kriyate tatra câ 'smadvyâkhyeyânâm tatra drishtânâm tadgranthaç ca, tataç ca nirvacanam upâdâya tad evâ 'smatprakaranânurûpam cet tadvat likhyate. Ananurûpam tu kimcid viparinamayya, anyeshâm ca katipayânâm niruktakâroktanirvacanasâmânyalaxanam anusritya niruktih kriyate. Nigamaç ca daxinâpathanivâsibhir adhîteshu vedeshu paridriçyamânas tattadbhâshyâni nirîxya tatra tatra pradarçyate. Adrishtanigamânâm ca padânâm ca bahuvedavidbhir nigamâ anveshyâh; ato 'smâbhir yathâmati pradarçitau pratipadanirvacananigamau vidvâmso buddhyâ nirûpya çukabhâshitavan manasi kurvantu*.

A few works are mentioned here which have not yet been discovered in India, but they are obviously of recent date. The confession of the utter inaccuracy of the texts, and of the loss of tradition, is of great importance, and ought to be always

* An abstract of this in German has already been given in Roth's Nirukta, pp. xlix. flg.

borne in mind by students of Vedic Literature, as a safeguard against the hasty acceptance of Vedic texts, to the authenticity of which not only intrinsic but extrinsic evidence also is wanting. It is impossible to doubt that all Indian books which have any pretence to antiquity have been worked over again and again, and in this process much must have been unwittingly falsified.

There are many other passages similar to the above which I could quote, but being by inferior and more recent writers, they would add nothing essential to the solution of the question. As a rule, the latest quote the most books, and there is often reason (e. g. Vâncheçvara's C. on the Hiranyakeçisûtra) to believe that they knew no more of them than the names.

A catalogue of the library that Sâyana *probably* possessed would be of great use, but after having noted all the writers he mentions in the published and MSS. works by him accessible to me, I have found it necessary to give up the enquiry, till the works of his predecessors (which he used so largely) can be thoroughly examined. Many (if not most) of Sâyana's quotations are what may be called traditional, and have been taken by him from the works of predecessors, not from original texts, and even in cases where he might have referred to the original. Two examples will suffice. In his Vyavahâramâdhava, his quotations are almost without exception taken from the Mitâxara, and as in the case of texts which still exist independently, his readings agree with those of the Mitâxarâ as opposed to the original works, he cannot even have verified his quotations. Again in the Sarvadarçanasangraha he appears to quote a large number of original works, but a great number of these quotations are second-hand. Thus in his account of *A*nandatîrtha's School* he quotes no less than eighteen original books, but only seven of these were really used by him, as I find by comparing MSS. of *A*nandatîrtha's works. In giving an abstract of the doctrine taught by this sectary, Sâyana adopted his quotations also. There is thus not the least reason to believe that even *A*nandatîrtha had before him the Bhâllaveyaçruti, the Çâkalyasa*m*hitâpariçish*t*a and similar Vedic works now lost, but from which he gives many passages. There is reason to believe that they will all be traced back to Ça*n*kara and still older compilers.†

Sâya*n*a's Commentaries are but poor testimony to the readings of the vedic texts current in his days. Where he copied his predecessors, as in his *R*igbhâshya, he no doubt gives the text as current hundreds of years before the dates at which we meet with MSS.; but he was very careless in many instances, notably in the Uttarârcika of the Sâmaveda, in which he adopted wholesale the readings of the *R*igveda, and neglected those of his text. A critical comparison of MSS. was and is still not appreciated by the Pandits.

Sâya*n*a's position is then almost precisely similar to that of the Alexandrian Neo-Platonists, and especially Proclus. Like him, Vidyâra*n*ya was a theosophist and hoped for the restoration by his mysteries of what was fast passing away. He was also, like Proclus, the representative of

---

*Pûr*n*apraj*n*adarçana, pp. 61, fg.

†The Mâdhavîyadhâtuvritti is, as regards quotations, perhaps the most interesting of all Vidyâra*n*ya's works, but it is for the above reason very difficult to deal with it satisfactorily. I must therefore defer to another occasion an enquiry as to what he intended by the Drâvida grammarians.

all the older science of his race, a philosopher, astronomer, philologist and mystic. Like him too he was a laborious painful compiler, whose industry supplied to some extent his lack of originality. The works of both therefore possess only an historical value, and are the best records of the last efforts of an old but decaying form of faith. As such, they call for editions which will preserve them for future enquirers into the history and philosophy of religions; but the work can be done only once for all time, and editors must therefore neglect no precaution to publish these difficult works in as thorough a way as they can with the materials available. That South-Indian and especially Telugu MSS. are the most trustworthy there can be no question. Sâyana was a Telugu brahman, and when he wrote his commentaries the old Telugu (or Halakannada) alphabet was the one he used. It is derived from the character used in the southern Açoka-inscriptions, and is the direct source of the modern Telugu and Canarese alphabets. The earliest forms of this important character are met with in the inscriptions of the Câlukya kings, and it was about 1000 A. D. used over greater part of the Deccan, and even as far south as Madras.* About the end of the 14th century the Devanâgarî alphabet was introduced, apparently by the followers of Anandatîrtha (Madhvâcârya), and was occasionally used for inscriptions on copper plates,† but

* At the Seven Pagodas. See the inscriptions in Major Carr's Collection of papers relating to that place. 8vo. Madras 1869.

†The Devanâgarî alphabet used in the kingdom of Vidyânagara in the 14th century is nearly precisely the same as that used at the same time in Northern India, but the practice of writing on palm leaves soon brought about a change in the form of the letters, and gave rise to the very illegible Nandinâgarî which has not differed since the 15th century, and is still much used by the followers of Anandatîrtha in the Mysore Country.

even these are attested in Halakannada. The MSS. in the Telugu character are therefore the nearest to what Vidyâranya's own autograph copy must have been. Abd-er-razzak tells us* that there were two kinds of materials used for writing in 1442 at Vidyânagara, leaves of palms and prepared cloth. The last is still much used for writing intended to be of only temporary use; it is prepared by smearing cotton cloth with a paste made of charcoal dust and the mucilage of tamarind seeds; it is folded in slips when dry, and then written on with either a pencil of steatite or of a compound of lead and tin which makes a white mark, and thus, a kadattam (as such a document is called) much resembles a slate. The palm leaves used are of the Palmyra (Borassus flabelliformis) or better still, the Talipot (Corypha umbraculifera);§ the last are especially durable. The letters are scratched on these slips of leaf with a heavy iron style, and the lines are then filled up and made visible with some black fluid. The kadattam is therefore suited for composition, and the ôlai or palm-leaf for making a fair copy of a finished work. The facsimile

---

*In Sir H. M. Elliot's "History of India" by Dowson, IV. pp. 107, 8. and also in Major's "India in the Fifteenth Century." (Hakluyt Society.)

"These people have two kinds of writing, one upon a leaf of the Hindî nut, which is two yards long, and two digits broad, on which they scratch with an iron style. These characters present no colour, and endure but for (108) a little while. In the second kind they blacken a white surface, on which they write with a soft stone cut into the shape of a pen, so that the characters are white on a black surface, and are durable. This kind of writing is highly esteemed."

This very excellent traveller is quite correct in his description except in the estimate of the value of either kind of material; in this respect the reverse of what he states is the case.

§By a curious oversight, Abd-er-razzak's editors state that the leaves alluded to are those of the coco-palm. This is quite incorrect; indeed its leaves are entirely unfit for such a purpose; nor is any kind of reed or flag used.

opposite will show what the original MSS. of Sâyaṇa's works were like, and will also give the Haḷaḱannaḍa alphabet.* That Sâyaṇa did actually use this character is shown by the errors of the Devanâgarî copies of his works. A notorious passage occurs in the Commentary on the *Ṛigveda*. (see Prof. Max Müller's *Ṛ*igvedasamhitâ, Vol. V. pp. xix. ffg.) which the editor has corrected and restored to what is, no doubt, its true form, but it is impossible to explain how the errors arose if Sâyaṇa used the Devanâgarî character. If however the passage be written in the Haḷakannaḍa, the origin of the numerous mistakes is at once apparent; a and â; û and dû, tha and jyâ; tha and dya; i and î and e; d and v; s and m, for example, being so very much alike that a Northerner who transcribed the original into Devanâgarî would be almost certain to err. Another source of error in the Devanâgarî transcripts is the S. Indian practice of assimilating visarga to a following sibilant and then doubling the latter. It is as well also to remark that the N. Indian transcripts have their own peculiar system of marking the accents; there are many systems used in Southern India which are entirely different.†

The great controversy‡ which has prevailed so long respect-

---

*It is the first page of Bhâvasena's Laghuvritti on the Kâtantra, and is the best and oldest specimen of a Haḷakannaḍa MSS. I could find, though only of about 1600. Nearly all the MSS. at Çringêri (I am told) are in the Haḷakannaḍa or (if recent) the Telugu character, and on palm leaves.

†Some are described in my "Catalogue" pp. 44, 5.

‡The question seems never to have occurred to Colebrooke, nor seriously to any one till Prof. Roth finally rejected Vidyâraṇya (Sâyaṇa) in his preface to the great "Wörterbuch" (I. p. v. 1855). Benfey in his "Sâmaveda" (1848) had, however, shown strong reasons for the same course. Stevenson in his translation of the same Veda published half a dozen years earlier, had implicitly followed Sâyaṇa, and so did Langlois in his *Ṛ*igveda. Prof. H. H. Wilson was also on the same side (*Ṛ*igvedasamhitâ (1860,

ಸ್ವಾದಿಷ್ಟಾಂಸುಲತ
ಧಗ್ಧಮಸ್ಕರ ಶಾಂ
ವಾಇಬಿಲಂಲ:೧
ಹಸಂಜ್ಞಾಹವಂ
ದ್ರಹ್ಮಾವಸ್ರಾಸ್ಪ
ಂಢೆಹಾಗಂದಮ
ಬಿಸಮಾನಸ್ಪುತಗ್ಣ

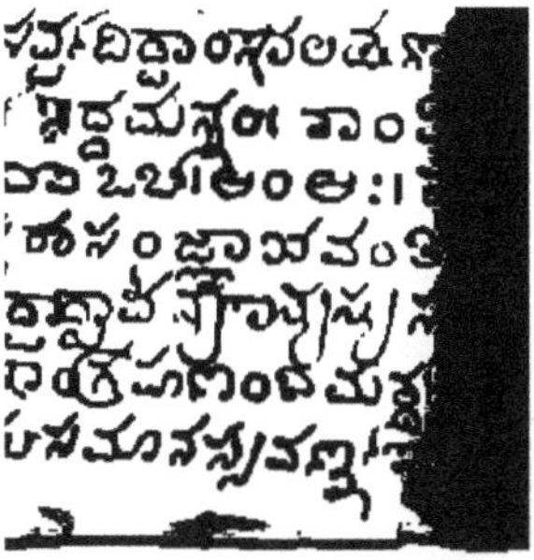

ing Sâyana's competence to explain the Vedas is fast approaching its end; the above sketch of his life and works will show that the followers of the "German School" are historically right. That they are so theoretically, is established by an amount of proof offered by Max Müller, Weber, Whitney, Roth, Muir and other that has long vanquished all reasonable hesitation on the part of the Sanskritists who once were inclined to prefer Sâyana and Indian precisians to the results of comparative philology.

But it must, however, never be forgotten that under the barbarian kings of Southern India, beginning with the Câlukyas, and continued by the Devagiri, Varangal and Vidyânagara dynasties, Sanskrit literature flourished more than it perhaps had ever done before, and that not only did this foreign civilization reduce Southern India to order, but even extended thence to the Malay Archipelago.* Sâyana as the typical re-

---

I., p. xlix, II, xviii. fg.); but Max Müller, Weber, Muir, and Whitney joined the opposite party. Prof. Goldstücker's "Pânini" (1861) urged all that could be said in favor of Sâyana, but since then Prof. Roth (Z. d. d. m. G. xxi., pp. 1—9), Prof. Whitney (Oriental and Linguistic Studies, pp. 100—132), Dr. Max Müller ("Hymns of the Gaupâyanas" in J. R. As. Soc. ii.) ("Rigveda" (tr.) I. p. viii. and fg.) have completely refuted the arguments of the conservative Sanskritists. What is really valuable in the Indian commentaries has been well pointed out by Dr. Haug (Ait. Br. I., pp. iv.—vi.) who is the advocate of a moderate course, in which Prof. Cowell appears to concur.

*It is well known that the Javanese civilization is said to have come from Kalinga (the Telugu country), and I think that there are ample reasons for believing that it was from the South of India rather than the North.

I. The Kawi is precisely analogous to the style introduced into Telugu by the grammarians of the 10th century, who tell us that their object was to teach how to write Kâvyas.

II. The old Javanese alphabet is closely connected with the early *Hala-kannada*, but not with those current in N. India.

III. Sanskrit words in Javanese and Kawi present Dravidianized forms, *e. g.* estri for stri.

presentative of this foreign culture must always remain an important figure in Indian history; in reducing, however, his claims to be heard as a scholar, there is much danger lest his importance in other respects be overlooked.

II.

The Vamçabrâhmana consists of a mere list of names of the succession of teachers of the Sâmaveda, but though the lowest names have the appearance of being those of authentic and historical personages, yet it is impossible to connect them with any definite period, and the highest names on the other hand are purely mythological. This list is therefore chiefly interesting on account of the numerous examples it gives of proper names as used by the ancient people that actually spoke Sanskrit, and thus also for the light it throws incidentally on their customs in this respect.

The names in this list are similar to those for the formation of which Pânini* and the older Grammarians give rules, and many

---

IV. There are Dravidian words in Javanese, *e. g.* tingal originally "moon" which is a pure Dravidian word.*

V. The Architecture of the Javanese temples closely resembles that of the Tamil temples. It has been erroneously restored by Raffles.

VI. The Kawi literature includes *Agamas*, which are peculiar to S. Indian Çaivism.

Many more such prima-facie reasons could be urged. It is to be hoped that the Dutch Sanskritists will not overlook the S. Indian literature.

*The sûtras quoted (from Pânini) by Sâyana are:

I., 2, 49 (p. 6); II., 4, 64 (4); III., 1, 69 (3); —, —, 138 (7); IV., 1, 81 (4); — — 96 (4, 11); — — 101 (8); — — 105 (3, 6); — — 112 (5); — — 122 (8); — 3, 30 (7); — — 84 (6); — — 120 (8); V., 4, 88 (6); — — 182 (6); VI., 3, 9 (7). Of other works he quotes the Mânavadh. ç. (II., 140 on p. 2); the Taittirîyâ (Kâthaka, XXIII., 6) on p. 2, and there is on the same page an anonymous quotation.

---

*Roorda explains this word by "onderdom der maan." (p. 112.)

are actually mentioned by not only Pâṇini but also by the Jain grammar attributed to Çâkṭâyana;* but it is impossible to bring them into harmony with the other Indian traditions† regarding the Vedas. The theory that the texts were seen by different Rishis is obviously inconsistent with the Vaṁça-brâhmaṇa which describes the handing down of the Sâma-veda as a whole, in which respect it approaches the Puranic legends. This succession of teachers is again utterly different from that in the Sâmavidhânabrâhmaṇa,‡ or the Çata-pathabrâhmaṇa; nor has it any connection with the Çâkhâ theory. The history of the collection and arrangement of the Vedic saṁhitâs and Brâhmaṇas is as yet hopelessly concealed by the dust of Indian fable; but as modern philology restores, though by mere fragments, the true picture of the ancient Indian world, our view of the part taken in succession by each Indian sect in obscuring the facts, will become defined, and it will then be possible to say which of the numerous sects who, in India, have successively sought after "religious merit" rather than facts, have added the incongruous elements now parts of the Veda, and to which sect each

---

*Many sûtras are almost absolutely the same in both grammars, *e. g.* "Gargâdibhyo yañ" (P. iv., 1, 105)="Gargâder yañ" (Çâk. ii., 4, 88); so "amâvâsyâyâ vâ" (P. iv., 3, 30)=Çâk. iii., 1, 94. In other cases what is contained in one sûtra of Pâṇini is split up into two or more by Çâkaṭâyana, and in some cases the last forms sûtras out of vârttikas or the words of the Mahâbhâshya; *e. g.* "atharvaṇo'ṇ" (iii., 1, 151) to supply a word not noticed by Pâṇini, âtharvaṇa, and which is based on Patañjali's C. on Pâṇini, iv., 3, 133. It is to be hoped that Dr. Bühler's long promised edition of Çâkaṭâyana will soon be available.

†Other notices of some of the names which occur in the text are given by Prof. Weber I. S. iv. pp., 375—386.

‡See my edition of the Sâmavidhânabrâhmaṇa, I., p. 101.

theory regarding the origin and collection of the Vedas is to be attributed.* Nor is it necessary to go back to almost prehistoric times in India to find material changes in what is esteemed the sacred literature; the Vedic canon is the work almost entirely of the modern sects beginning with the followers of Çankarâcârya, and it is by comparing their statements with the Veda before us, that we must begin the enquiry how it happened that the Veda exists in its present form. The latest changes are obviously those of mere arrangement; the grammarians and etymologists preserved the texts to a certain extent, but far from intact. If Yâska's collection of obsolete words was collected from the Vedic texts of his day, how is it that the best informed commentators have long failed to discover passages in the existing Vedic works which justify the words he gives? If one considers the order of the eight Brâhmanas of the Sâma Veda, it is very plain that Sâyana considered them to be parts of a whole, and thus his commentaries would tend to fuse them into one like the Çatapathabrâhmana which contains both Brâhmana and Aranyakâ Sections.

The text of the Vamçabrâhmana has already been edited by Prof. A. Weber in his "Indische Studien" (IV. pp. 271-386), and I have marked his readings (which are based on two MSS. from Northern India) by W. I have also been able to collate two South Indian MSS., Tanjore, No. 2,516 (=A.) and do. No. 9,028 (=B); the first in Devanâgari and the last in

*Nearly all the Indian views regarding the origin and collections of the Vedas are to be found in Dr. Muir's "Original Sanskrit Texts" vol. III., but I am not aware that the influence of these views that prevailed at different times has ever been insisted on in regard to the present state of the texts.

the Grantha character, neither more than a century old. For the Commentary, I used a very accurate G r a n t h a MS. belonging to a Brahman in the Tanjore District, and also had for the first few pages a transcript I made of the beginning of the MS. described in my "Catalogue" (p. 52) and now in the Library of the India Office, London. Where I have introduced any change, I have (however trifling it be) marked it with ( ). The *text* is that of Sâ y a *n* a, various readings are given below.

The system of transliteration adopted is:

a, â (and for typographical reasons *A*) i, î, u, û, ri, e, ai, o, au.
k kh g gh *n* (and ṅ)
c ch j jh *n* (and ṅ)
t *t*h *d* *d*h *n* (and ṇ)
p ph b bh m
y r l v ç sh s h *l*.
anusvâra is expressed by *m*, and visarga by *h*.

ATHA

VA*M*ÇABRĀHMA*N*ABĀSHYAM |

Vâgîçâdyâ*h* sumanasa*h* sarvârthânâm upakrame |
ya*m* natvâ k*r*itak*r*ityâ*h* syus ta*m* namâmi gajânanam || 1 ||
yasya niçvasita*m* vedâ yo vedebhyo 'khila*m* jagat |
nirmame tam aha*m* vande vidyâtîrtha*m* maheçvaram || 2 ||
tatka*t*âxe*n*a tadrûpa*m* dadhad Bukka-mahîpati*h* |
âdiçat Sâya*n*âcârya*m* vedârthasya prakâçane || 3 ||
ye pûrvottaramîmâ*m*se te vyâkhyâyâ 'tisangrahât |
k*r*ipâlu*h* Sâya*n*âcâryo vedârtha*m* vaktum udyata*h* || 4 ||
vyâkhyâtâv *r*igyajurvedau sâmavede 'pi sa*m*hitâ |
vyâkhyâtâ, brâhma*n*asyâ 'tha vyâkhyâna*m* sampravartate || 5 ||
ash*t*au hi brâhma*n*agranthâ*h* prau*d*ha*m* brâhma*n*am âdimam |
sha*d*vi*m*çâkhya*m* dvitîya*m* syât tata*h* sâmavidhir bhavet || 6 ||
ârsheya*m* devatâdhyâyo bhaved upanishat tata*h* |
sa*m*hitopanishad va*m*ço granthâ ash*t*âv itî 'ritâ*h* || 7 ||
prau*d*hâdibrâhma*n*âny âdau sapta vyâkhyâya çântimam |
va*m*çâkhya*m* brâhma*n*a*m*[1] vidvân Sâya*n*o vyâcikîrshati || 8 ||

Asmin brâhma*n*e k*r*itsnasâmavedâdhyet*r*î*n*â*m* prav*r*ittirucy-utpâdanâya sampradâyapravartakâ *r*ishaya*h* prad*r*içyante | tatra prathama*m* sarvatra granthâdau parâparagurunamaskâra*h* kartavya iti sûcayitum brahmâdiparâparagurunamaskâra*m* darçayati | "namo brahma*n*e namo brâhma*n*ebhyo nama âcâryebhyo nama *r*ishibhyo namo devebhyo namo vâyave ca m*r*ityave ca vish*n*ave ca namo vaiçrava*n*âya ca" iti | 'brahma*n*e' mahate svaya*m*bhuve

[1] C. va*m*çâkhyabrâhma*n*am |

o*m* nama*h* sâmavedâya | [1]

o*m*[2] namo brahma*n*e, namo brâhma*n*ebhyo,
nama âcâryebhyo, nama *r*ishibhyo, namo
devebhyo, namo vedebhyo, namo vâyave

carâcarâtmakasya sarvasya jagato vidhâtre 'nama*h*' namaskâro bhavatu | tathâ 'brâhma*n*ebhya*h*' | brahma*n*â vedenâ 'nantena cesh*t*ena nityanaimittikâdîni karmâ*n*i kurvantî 'ti brâhma*n*â*h* | yad vâ brahmâ 'dhîyate vidanti vâ brâhma*n*â*h* | brahma*n*o 'patyâni vâ brâhma*n*âs tebhyo 'nama*h*' devebhyo 'pi pûrva*m* brâhma*n*anamaskâras tesh*â*m brâhma*n*âdhînatvapradarçanârtha*h* | tathâ t a i t t i r î y â âmananti—"yâvatîr vai devatâs tâ*h* sarvâ vedavidi brâhma*n*e vasanti | tasmâd brâhma*n*ebhyo vedavidbhyo dive dive namaskuryân nâ 'çlîla*m* kîrtayed etâ eva devatâ*h* prî*n*âti" iti[3] | smaranti ca—

"daivâdhîna*m* jagat sarva*m* mantrâdhîna*m* tu daivatam |
tan mantra*m* brâhma*n*âdhînam brâhma*n*o nama devatâ" ||

iti[4] | tathâ 'âcâryebhya*h*'—

"upanîya tu ya*h* çishya*m* vedam adhyâpayed dvija*h* |
sakalpa*m* sarahasya*m* ca tam âcâryam pracaxate" || [5]

ity uktalaxa*n*â âcâryâs tebhyo 'nama*h*' | tathâ '*r*ishibhyo nama*h*' | *r*ishibhya*h* atîndriyârthadarçibhya*h* | sâmavedadrash*t*ribhyo gautamâdibhyo nama*h* | tathâ 'devebhya*h*' | divyantî 'ti devâ*h* | dyotanâdigu*n*ayuktebhya indrâdibhyo 'nama*h*' | 'vâyave' ca sarvajagatprâ*n*abhûtâya devâya 'nama*h*' | 'm*r*ityave' sarvajagata*h* sa*m*hartre etannâmakâya devâya nama*h* | 'vish*n*ave ca' sarvavyâpakâya paramâtmarûpâya 'nama*h*' | tathâ 'vaiçrava*n*âya' devâya nama*h* | viçravaso 'patya*m* vaiçrava*n*a*h* | "d i v â d i-

---

[1] & [2]) om. A. B. C[a].

[3]) According to the St. Petersburg Lexicon (s. v. 'açlîla') this quotation is from the Kâ*th*aka. (23, 6.)

[4]) I cannot identify this piece of insolence. It is always in the mouths of S. Indian Brahmans.

[5]) Mânava-dh: ç: ii., 140.

ca, mrityave ca, vishnave ca,
namo vaiçravanâya ca, 'pajâyata[1])
çarvadattâd gârgyâc[2]), charvadatto[1])
gârgyo [2]) rudrabhûter drâhyâyanâd[3])
[3]) rudrabhûtir drâhyâyanas [4]) trâtâd

bhyah" iti "çyan" (P. iii., 1, 69) | yadyapi 'namo devebhyah' ity anenai 'va vâyvâdînâm api namaskâra uktah | tathâ 'pi prithannirdeço 'tra teshâm prâdhânyapradarçanârthah | prâdhânyam ca teshâm jagannirvâhakatvât | evam parâparagurunamaskâram darçayitve 'dânîm sampradâyapravartakân rishîn darçayitum upakramate | "upajâyata" | upasargavaçâd arthântaram | sângam sâmavedam adhyaishta adhîtavân | brâhmanânâm dvijanma dvayena bhâvyam | ekam janma çuklaçonitasambhûtam | ritumâtrâsamyuktam çuklam çariram janayati | tat prathamam janma | dvitîyam tu vidyâjanma mâtâ gâyatrî pitâ hy âcâryah | athâ 'câryaparamparâm âha | 'çarvadattâd gârgyât' ityâdinâ | 'çarvadattâd gârgyât' ity ârabhya â 'brahmano vamçam anukrâmet' | 'gârgyât' gargasya gotrâpatyam gârgyah | "gargâdibhyo yañ (P. iv., 1, 105) | çarvadattah çarvena dattah çarva[5]) îçvarah | etannâmakâd risher 'upajâyata' sâmavedam adhyaishta | bahulakâd adabhâvah | "çarvadatto gârgyo rudrabhûter drâhyâyanât" iti | gârgyah çarvadatto 'pi 'drâhyâyanât' drahyasyâ 'patyât | drahyaçabdâd[6]) "gargâdibhyah" iti yañi krite "yañiñoç ca" iti phak (P. iv., 1, 101) | rudrabhûtinâmakâd risher gârgyah sâmavedam adhyaishta |

---

[1]) Profr. Weber reads—upajâya ca—on the authority of 2 MSS. I suggested Sâyana's reading was more correct ("Catalogue," p. 52); but in a letter (d. 24. July 1871) to me he condemns this reading as unusual and improbable, and in a review of my Catalogue (Lit. Centralbl.) he says: "Die auf p. 52 gerügte Lesart upajâya ca im Eingang des Vamçabrâhmana hat sich schliesslich doch wieder als berechtigt erwiesen." A. B. co 'pajâyata.

[2]) W. gârgyâ. [3]) B. W. drâhyâyana. [4]) A. W. drâhyâyanis. [5]) C. Cr. çarvadatta. [6]) om. C.

aishumatât, 4) trâta aishumato nigadât[1] pârnavalker,
5) nigadah [2]pârnavalkir giriçarmanah kânthevidher,[3]
6) giriçarmâ kântheviddhir[4] brahmavriddheç chandoga-

evam sarvatra yojanîyam | 'rudrabhûtir drâhyâyanas trâtâd aishumatât' iti | ishumato gotrâpatyât 'trâtât' etannâmakât | 'trâta aishumato nigadât pârnavalkeh' iti | trâto 'pi pârnavalkeh parnavalkasyâ 'patyât | "bâhvâdibhyaç ca" (P. iv., 1, 96) itî 'ñ | nigadanâmakât | "nigadah pârnavalkir giriçarmanah kântheviddheh" iti | "daivayajniçaucivrixisâtyamugrikântheviddhibhyo 'nyatarasyâm" (P. iv., 1, 81) ity apatyârtha iñantatvena nipâtitah | kântheviddhasyâ 'patyât giriçarmanâmakât | "giriçarmâ kântheviddhir brahmavriddheç chandogamâhakeh" iti | chandogamâhakasyâ 'patyam chandogamâhakih | sanjnâpûrvavidher anityatvâd vriddhyabhâvah | tasmâd brahmavriddhinâmakâd | brahmanâ vedena vardhata iti brahmavriddhih | "kticktau ca sanjnâyâm" (P. iii., 3, 174) iti ktic | "brahmavriddhiç chandogamâhakir mitravarcasah sthairakâyanât" iti | sthirakasya yuvâpatyât | sthirakaçabdâd iñantâd "yañiñoç ca" (P. iv., 1, 101) iti phak | tasmân mitravarcaso mitrasya sûryasya varca iva varco yasya sa mitravarcâs tannâmakât | "mitravarcâh sthairakâyanah supratîtâd aulundyât" iti | ulundasya gotrâpatyâd | ulundaçabdâd gotrâpatye yañ drashtavyah | tasmât supratîtât vikhyâte supratîtas tannâmakât | "supratîta aulundyo brihaspatiguptâc châyastheh" iti | brihaspatir iva vidyayâ guptas tannâmakât | "brihaspatiguptah çâyasthir bhavatrâtâc châyastheh" iti | çâyasther bhavene' çvarena trâto raxito bhavatrâtas tannâmakât | "bhavatrâtah çâyasthih kustukâc chârkarâxyât" iti | 'çârkarâxyât' çarkarâxasya gotrâpatyâd "gargâdibhya" iti yañ | tasmât kustukanâmakât | "kustukah çârkarâxyah çravanadattât kauhalât" iti | 'kauha-

1) B. nigadât. 2) B. nigadah. 3) B. vriddher. 4) B. vriddhir.

mâhaker 7) brahmav*r*idhhiç chandogamâhakir mitravarcasa*h*
sthairakâyanân, 8) mitravarcâ*h* sthairakâyana*h* supratîtâd
aulu*nd*yât, 9) supratîta aulu*nd*yo b*r*ihaspatiguptâc[1] châyasther, 10) b*r*ihaspatigupta*h* çâyasthir bhavatrâtâc châyasther,[2]
11) bhavatrâta*h* çâyasthi*h* kustukâc chârkarâxyât,[3]
12) kustuka*h* çârkarâxya*h*[4] çrava*n*adattât kauhalâc,
13) chrava*n*adatta*h*[5] kauhala*h* suçâradâc châlakâyanât,[6]
14) suçârada*h* çâlakâyana[7] ûrjayata aupamanyavât,
15) ûrjayann aupamanyavo bhânumata aupamanyavâd,
16) bhânumân aupamanyava ânandajâc cândhanâyanâd,

lât' kohalasyâ 'patyât | "çivâdibhyo 'a" (P. iv., 1, 112) ity a*n* | tasmât 'çrava*n*adattât' çrava*n*ena vidyayâ dattam dhana*m* yasya, tannâmakât | "çrava*n*adatta*h* kauhala*h* suçâradâc châlakâyanât" iti çalakor gotrâpatyât | çalaku*h* çala*m*kuç ce 'ti na*d*âdishu pâ*th*ât phak tatsanniyogenâ 'deçaç ca | tasmât 'suçâradât' çobhanâ*h* çâradâ yasye 'ti suçârada iti vigrahas tannâmakât | "suçârada*h* çâlakâyana ûrjayata aupamanyavât" iti upamanyor apatyâd 'ûrjayata*h*' vidyâtapobalavata ûrjayannâmakât | "ûrjayann aupamanyavo bhânumata aupamanyavât" iti | aupamanyavâd bhânumatas tejasvinas tannâmakât | "bhânumân aupamanyava ânandajâc cândhanâyanât" iti | 'cândhanâyanât' candhanasya yuvâpatyât | candhanaçabdâd ira*n*tâd "yaña*n*oç ca" iti phak | tasmâd ânanda*m* janayatî 'ty ânandajas tannâmakât | "ânandajaç cândhanâyana*h* çâmbâc chârkarâxyât kâmbojâc c' aupamanyavât" iti | 'çârkarâxyât' çarkarâxasya gotrâpatyât 'çâmba'-nâmakâd *r*ishe*h* | 'aupamanyavât' upamanyor apatyât kâmbojanâmakâd *r*isheç c' ânandajo vidyâta upajâyata | "çâmba*h* çârkarâxya*h* kâmbojaç c' aupamanyavo madrakârâc chaungâyane*h*" iti | 'çaungâyane*h*' çaungâyanasyâ 'pat-

---

1) A. W. °guptâ châ° 2) W. °trâtâ châ°.
3) W. kustukâ chârkarâxât. 4) W. çârkarâxa*h*. 5) W. kauhalâ chra°. 6) W. suçâradâ châlamkâyanât. A. B. châlamkâ°. 7) A. B. W. çâlamkâyana.

17) ânandajaç cândhanâyanah çâmbâo[1] chârkarâxyât[2] kâmbojâo c' aupamanyavâo[3] 18) châmbah çârkarâxyah[4] kâmbojâo c' aupamanyavo madrakârâc[5] chaungâyaner 19) madrakârah[6] çaungâyanih svâter[7] aushtrâxeh 20) svâtir[8] aushtrâxih suçravaso vârshaganyât, 21) suçravâ vârshaganyah prâtarahnât kauhalât, 22) prâtarahnah kauhalah ketor vâjyât, 23) ketur vâjyo mitravindât kauhalân, 24) mitravindah

yât | phagantâd apatyârtha in | tasmân madrakâranâmakâd rishes tâv ubhâv api vidyâta upâjanishâtâm ity arthah | "madrakâraç çaungâyanih svâter aushtrâxeh" iti | aushtrâxer ushtrâxasyâ 'patyât 'svâteh' svâtinaxatre jâtah svâtih | "çravishthâphalgunyanurâdhâsvâtî"-'tyâdinâ (P. iv., 3, 34) naxatragatasyâ 'no luk tasmin krite "luk taddhitaluki" (P. i., 2, 49) iti strîpratyayasyâ 'pi lug bhavati | tannâmakâd risheh | "svâtir aushtrâxih suçravaso vârshaganyât" iti | 'vârshaganyât' vrishaganyasya gotrâpatyât | vrishaganaçabdât "gargâdibhyo yan" (P. iv., 1 | 105) tasmât 'suçravasah' sushthu çravo yasya tannâmakât | "suçravâ vârshaganyah prâtarahnât kauhalât" iti | 'kauhalât' kohalasyâ 'patyât 'prâtarahnât' prâtarahni bhavah prâtarâhnah | etannâmakâd risheh | "ahno 'hna etebhyah" (P. v., 4, 88) ity avyayâd uktasyâ 'han-çabdasyâ 'hnâdeçah | "prâtarahnah kauhalah ketor vâjyât" iti | 'vâjyât' vâjasya gotrâpatyât 'ketoh' tannâmakât | "ketur vâjyo mitravindât kauhalât" iti | 'mitravindât kauhalât' mitrâni vindatî 'ti mitravindah tannâmakât "gavâdishu vindeh sanjnâyâm (upasankhyânam" P. iii., 1, 138 v.) iti vârttikakâravacanân mitropapadâd vindeh çapratyayah | "mitravindah kauhalah sunîthât kâpatavât" iti | 'kâpatavât' kapator apatyât çobhanavacanah 'sunîthah' etannâmakâd risheh |

---

1) A. W. çâmbâ. 2) A. W. chârkarâxât. 3) A. W. aupamanyavâ—. 4) A. W. çârkarâxah. 5) A. B. W. madragârâ. 6) A. B. W. madragârah. 7) A. W. sâter. 8) A. W. sâtir.

kauhala*h* sunîthât kâpa*t*avât, 25) sunîtha*h* kâpa*t*ava*h* sutemanasa*h* çâ*nd*ilyâyanât, 26) sutemanâ*h* çâ*nd*ilyâyano '*m*çor dhâna*n*jayyâd 27) a*m*çur dhâna*n*jayya*h* ‖ 1 ‖ amâvâsyâc[1]) châ*nd*ilyâyanâd râdhâc ca gautamâd, 28) râdho gautamo gâtur gautamât pitur, 29) gâtâ gautama*h* sa*m*vargajito lâmakâyanât, 30) sa*m*vargajil lâmakâyana*h* çâkadâsâd bhâ*d*itâ-

"sunîtha*h* kâpa*t*ava*h* sutemanasa*h* çâ*nd*ilyâyanât" iti | 'çâ*nd*ilyâyanât' çâ*nd*ilyasya gotrâpatyam çâ*nd*ilyas tasyâ 'patyât | gargâdipâ*t*hâd ya*ñ* tadantât phak | tasmât 'sutemanasa*h*' sute abhishute some mano yasya sa sutemanâ*h* | tannâmakât "haladantât saptamyâ*h* sa*m*jnâyâm" (P. vi., 3, 9) ity aluk | "sutemanâ*h* çâ*nd*ilyâyano '*m*çor dhâna*n*jayyât" iti | 'dhâna*n*jayyât' dhana*n*jayasya gotrâpatyât | gargâdishu pâ*t*hâd ya*ñ* | tasmâd a*m*ços tannâmakât sutemanâ adhyaish*t*a | "a*m*çur dhâna*n*jayya*h*" | ity uttarakâ*nd*açesho 'yam ‖ Iti va*m*çabrâhma*n*e prathama*h* kha*nd*a*h* ‖

2. "Amâvâsyâc câ*nd*ilyâyanâd râdhâc ca gautamât" iti | dhâna*n*jayyo '*m*çu*h* çâ*nd*ilyâyanâd amâvâsyâyâ*m* jâto 'mâvâsya*h* "amâvâsyâyâ vâ" (P. iv., 3, 30) ity akârapratyaya*h* | tannâmakâd *r*ishe*h* "gautamât" gotamasya gotrâpatyât 'râdhât' etannâmakâd *r*isheç ca vidyâta upajâyata | "gautamo râdho gautamâd gâtu*h*" sâmagânaçîlâd etannâmakât pitur evâ 'dhyaish*t*a | "gâtâ gautama*h* sa*m*vargajito lâmakâyanât" iti | 'lâmakâyanât' lâmakasya yuvâpatyât sa*m*vargajinnâmakâd *r*ishe*h* | "sa*m*vargajil lâmakâyana*h* çâkadâsâd bhâ*d*itâyanât" iti | bha*d*itasyâ 'patya*m* bhâ*d*iti*h* | tasyâ 'patya*m* bhâ*d*itâyana*h* tasmât | çakyate samâdhinâ 'vagantum iti çâka*h* îçvara*h* tasya dâsa*h* 'çâkadâsa*h*' tannâmakât | "çâkadâso bhâ*d*itâyano vica*ks*a*n*at tâ*nd*yât" iti

1) *W.* amâvâsyâ.

yanâc,[1] 31) châkadâso bhâ*d*itâyano vicaxa*n*ât tâ*nd*yâd,
32) vicaxa*n*as tâ*nd*yo gardabhîmukhâc châ*nd*ilyâyanâd,
33) gardabhîmukha*h* çâ*nd*ilyâyana udaraçâ*nd*ilyât pitur,
34) udaraçâ*nd*ilyo 'tidhanvanaç ca çaunakân maçakâc
ca gârgyân, 35) maçako gârgya*h* sthirakâd gârgyât

'tâ*nd*yât' ta*nd*asya gotrâpatyât gargâditvâd yañ | tasmâd vicaxa*n*anâmakât | "vicaxa*n*as tâ*nd*yo gardabhîmukhâc châ*nd*ilyâyanât" iti | çâ*nd*ilyasyâ 'patyât 'gardabhîmukha-'nâmakât | "gardabhîmukha*h* çâ*nd*ilyâyana udaraçâ*nd*ilyât pitu*h*" iti | so 'py 'udaraçâ*nd*ilyât' | udaraçabdena santatir laxyate bahusantânata*h* çâ*nd*ilyât 'pitu*h*' evâ 'dhyaish*t*a | udaraçâ*nd*ilyo 'tidhanvanaç ca çaunakân masakâc ca gârgyat" iti | udaraçâ*nd*ilyo 'pi 'çaunakât' çaunakanâmakasya 'rsher gotrâpatyât— "çaunakâdibhyo 'ñ | tasmât 'atidhanvana*h*' dhanur ity âyudhamâtrasyo 'palaxa*n*a*m* tad atikrânta*m* yena tannâmakât | bahuvrîhau 'dhanushaç ca' (P. v., 4, 132) ity anañ | 'gârgyât'— gargasya gotrâpatyât | 'maçakâc ca' vidyâta upajâyata | ubhayatrâ 'pi cakâra itaretarasamuccayârtha*h* | "maçako gârgya*h* sthirakâd gârgyât pitu*h*" iti | gârgyo maçakas tu gârgyât sthirakanâmakât pitur evâ 'dhyaish*t*a | "sthirako gârgyo vâsish*t*hâc caikitâneyât" iti | 'vâsish*t*hât' vasish*t*asyâ 'patyât 'caikitâneyât' etannâmakât | "vâsish*t*haç caikitâneyo vâsish*t*hâd âraiha*n*yâd râjanyât" iti | 'vâsish*t*hât' vasish*t*hasyâ 'patyâd âraiha*n*yanâmakâd 'râjanyât' rishe*h* | mukhyasya râjanyasyâ 'dhyâpana adhikârâsa*m*bhavât | "vâsish*t*ha âraiha*n*ya râjanya*h* sumantrâd bâbhravâd gautamât" iti | 'gautamât' gotamasa*m*bandhina*h* "tasye 'dam" (P. iv., 3, 120) ity aṇ | 'bâbhravât' babhror apatyât sumantranâmakâd *r*ishe*h* | "sumantro bâbhravo gautama*h* çûshâd vâhneyâd bhâradvâjât" iti | 'bhâradvâjât' bharadvâjasa*m*bandhino 'vâhneyât' vahner apatyât "itaçcânina*h*" (P. iv., 1, 122) iti *d*hak | tasmât 'çûsha'—nâmakât |

1) W. °nâ—.

pitu*h*, 36) sthirako gârgyo vâsish*t*hâc caikitâneyâd 37) vâsish*t*haç caikitâneyo vâsish*t*hâd âraiha*n*yâd[1] râjanyâd, 38) vâsish*t*ha âraiha*n*yo[2] râjanya*h* sumantrâd bâbhravâd gautamât, 39) sumantro bâbhravo gautama*h* çûshâd vâhneyâd bhâradvâjâc,[3] 40) chûsho vâhneyo bhâradvâjo 'râlâd dârteyâc[4] chaunakâd, 41) arâlo dârteya*h* çaunako d*r*iter aindrotâc[5] chaunakât pitur, 42) d*r*itir aindrota*h* çaunaka indrotâc[6] chaunakât pitur eve 43) 'ndrota*h* çaunako v*r*ishaçûsh*n*âd vâtâvatâd, 44) v*r*ishaçûsh*n*o vâtâvato nikothakâd bhâyajâtyân, 45) nikothako bhâyajâtya*h* pratither devatarathât, 46) pratithir devataratho devatarasa*h* çâvasâyanât pitur, 47) devatarâ*h* çâvasâyana*h* çavasa*h* pitur eva, 48) çavâ agnibhuva*h* kâçya-

"çûsho vâhneyo bhâradvâjo 'râlâd dârteyâc chaunakât" iti | 'çaunakât' çunakasa*m*bandhino 'dârteyât' d*r*iter apatyâd arâlanâmakât | "arâlo dârteya*h* çaunako d*r*iter aindrotâc chaunakât pitu*h*" iti | çaunakât 'aindrotât' indrotasyâ 'patyâd d*r*iter etannâmakât 'pitur' eva | "d*r*itir aindrota*h* çaunaka indrotâc chaunakât pitur eva" iti | 'çaunakât' çunakagotrâpatyât 'indrotât' tannâmakât pitur evâ 'dhyaish*t*a | "indrota*h* çaunako v*r*ishaçûsh*n*âd vâtâvatât" iti | 'vâtâvatât' vatâvatasyâ 'patyât v*r*ishaçûsh*n*anâmakât | "v*r*ishaçûsh*n*o vâtâvato nikothakâd bhâyajâtyât" iti | bhayajâtasya gotrâpatyân nikothakanâmakât | "nikothako bhâyajâtya*h* pratither devatarathât" iti | 'devatarathât' devân yaj*n*ena taratî 'ti 'devataratha*h*' tasyâ 'patyât 'pratithe*h*' prak*r*ish*t*âs tithayo yasya sarvartushu yâgâdipu*n*yakarme 'ty artha*h* | tannâmakât | "pratithir devataratho devata-

1) C[1]. âraihanyâd. B. âraibi°. 2) C[2]. âraibanyo. B. âraibi°. 3) W. bhâradvâjâ—. 4) W. dâureya*h*. He suggests however the correct reading as above. A. dâure°. 5) W. aindrotâ. 6) W. indrotâ.

pâd, 49) agnibhûh kâçyapa indrabhuvah kâçyapâd, 50) indrabhûh kâçyapo mitrabhuvah kâçyapân, 51) mitrabhûh kâçyapo vibhandakât kâçyapât pitur, 52) vibhandakah kâçyapa rishyaçringât[1] kâçyapât pitur, 53) rishyaçringah kâçyapah kaçyapât pitur eva, 54) kaçyapo 'gner, 55) agnir indrâd, 56) indro vâyor, 57) vâyur mrityor, 58) mrityuh prajâpateh, 59) prajâpatir brahmano, 60) brahmâ svayambhûs, tasmai namas tebhyo namah || 2 ||

rasah çâvasâyanât pituh" iti | 'çâvasâyanât' çavaso 'patyât 'devatarasah' etannâmakât pitur eva | "devatarâh çâvasâyanah çavasah pitur eva" iti | so 'pi 'çavasah' tannâmakât pitur evâ 'dhitavân | "çavâ agnibhuvah kâçyapât" iti | 'kâçyapât' kaçyapagotrotpannât 'agnibhuvah' agner bhavati 'ty agnibhûh | tannâmakât çavo 'ta vidyâta upajâyata | "agnibhûh kâçyapa indrabhuvah kâçyapât" iti | indrâd bhavati 'ty 'indrabhûh' tannâmakât | "indrabhûh kâçyapa mitrabhuvah kâçyapât" iti | mitrât sûryâd bhavati 'ti "mitrabhûh" tannâmakât | "mitrabhûh kâçyapo vibhandakât kâçyapât pituh" iti | kaçyapagotrâpatyâd api 'vibhandakât' etannâmakât pitur eva | "vibhandakah kâçyapa rishaçringât[1] kâçyapât pituh" iti | 'kâçyapât' kaçyapâpatyâd rishyaçringanâmakâd risher pitur eva vibhandako 'dhitavân | "rishyaçringah kâçyapah kaçyapât pitur eva" iti | so 'pi kaçyapât pitur evâ 'dhyaishta | "kaçyapo 'gneh" iti | 'kaçyapa 'gneh' devatâyâ vidyâta upajâyata | "agnir indrât" iti | agniç ce 'ndrâd devât | "indro vayoh" iti | 'vâyoh' sarvajagatprânâtmakâd indro 'dhitavân | "vâyur mrityoh" iti | 'vâyur mrityoh' devât | "mrityuh prajâpateh" iti | so 'pi 'prajâpateh' carâcarâtmakasya jagatah srashtuh | "prajâpatir brahmanah" iti | 'brahmanah' mahatah svayambhuvah sakâçât sângam sâmavedam adhîtavân | "brahmâ svayambhûh" iti | sa tu svayamprabhâtavidyatvân nâ 'nyasmâd adhyaishte 'ty arthah ||

[1] C. riçya°.

**âcâryebhyo namaskritvâ 'tha vamçasya kîrtayet |
svadhâ pûrveshâm bhavati netâ 'yur dîrgham açnute ||
ity uktvâ 'nukrâmed vamçam â brahmano nayann 1) arya-
mabhûtah kâlabavâd, 2) aryamabhûtih kâlabavo bhadraçar-
manah kauçikâd, 3) bhadraçarmâ kauçikah pushyayaçasa
audavrajeh, 4) pushyayaçâ audavrajih samkarâd gautamât,
5) samkaro gautamo 'ryamarâdhâc ca gobhilât pûshamitrâc**

Evam vidyâsampradâyapravartakân rishîn devatâmç ca darçayitve 'dânîm ante 'pi parûparagurunamaskâran darçayati "tasmai namas tebhyo namah" iti | 'tasmai' svayambhuve brahmane 'namah' | 'tebhyah' pûrvoktebhyah namah ||

|| Iti vamçabrâhmanabhâshye dvitîyah khandah ||

3. Evam sâmavedasampradâyapravartakâm ekâm rishiparamparâm darçayitvâ parâm api darçayitum tatkîrtane kincin niyamam darçayati | "âcâryebhyo namaskritvâ. . . . . â brahmanah" iti | atha yathoktavamçakîrtanânantaram vamçasyâ 'nyasya 'rshîn kîrtayet 'âcâryebhyah' brahmâdibhyo 'namaskritvâ' | 'pûrveshâm' pitrâdibhyah | caturthyarthe shashthî | 'svadhâ' kavyam dattam 'bhavati' bhavatu | 'netâ' sampradâyapravartaka etatsamjnaka rishir 'dîrgham âyur açnuta' ity etanmantram uktvâ 'â brahmanah' brahmaparyantam 'vamçam anukrâmet' kîrtayet | yadartham niyamo darçitas tam vaktum upakram[at]e ; "nayann aryamabhûteh kâlabavât" iti | sâmasampradâyapravartako nayannâma 'rshih 'kâlabavât' kâlabavasyâ 'patyât 'aryamabhûteh' aryamenâ 'bhûtir iva bhûtir yasya tannâmakâd risher vidyâta upajâyate 'ti çeshah | "aryamabhûtih kâlabhavo bhadraçarmanah kauçikât" iti | so 'pi 'kauçikât' kuçikasyâ 'patyât 'bhadraçarmanah' bhadram kalyânam çarmasthânam yasya tannâmakât | "bhadraçarmâ kauçikah pushyayaçasa audavrajeh" iti | 'audavrajeh' udavrajasyâ 'patyât "bahvâdibhyaç ca" (P. iv., 1, 45) iti iñ | pushyayaçasa iva yaço yasya tannâmakât | "pushyayaçâ audavrajih samkarâd gauta-

ca gobhilât, 6)pûshamitro gobhilo 'çvamitrâd gobhilâd, 7)açvamitro gobhilo varu*n*amitrâd gobhilâd, 8)varu*n*amitro gobhilo mûlamitrâd gobhilân, 9)mûlamitro gobhilo vatsamitrâd gobhilâd, 10)vatsamitro gobhilo gaulgulavîputrâd gobhilâd, 11)gaulgulavîputro gobhilo b*r*ihadvaso*h* pitur, 12)b*r*ihadvasur gobhilo gobhilâd eva, 13)gobhilo râdhâc ca gautamâd |

samâna*m* para*m* samânam param || 3 ||

|| Iti va*m*çabrâhma*n*a*m* samâptam ||

mât" iti | 'gautamât' gotamasyâ 'patyât sa*m*karanâmakât | "sa*m*karo gautamo 'ryamarâdhâc ca gobhilât pûshamitrâc ca gobhilât" iti | 'gobhilât' gobhilâpatyâd 'aryamarâdhât' aryamna*h* sa*m*jâto 'râdha*h*' siddhir yasya tannâmakâd gobhilât 'pûshamitrât' pûshâ devo mitra*m* yasya tannâmakâd *r*isheç ca vidyâta upajâyata | "pûshamitro gobhilo 'çvamitrâd gobhilât" iti | 'gobhilât' açvamitranâmakâd *r*ishe*h* pûshamitro 'dhyaish*t*a | "açvamitro gobhilo varu*n*amitrâd gobhilât" iti | varu*n*o mitra*m* yasya tannâmna*h* | "varu*n*amitro gobhilo mûlamitrâd gobhilât" iti mûlamitranâmakât | "mûlamitro gobhilo vatsamitrâd gobhilât" iti | gobhilasa*m*bandhino vatsamitrât vatso nâma '*r*shir mitra*m* yasya tasmât | "vatsamitro gobhilo gaulgulavîputrâd gobhilât" iti | gulgulor apatya*m* strî gaulgulavî tasyâ*h* putrâd gobhilât | "gaulgulavîputro gobhilo b*r*ihadvaso*h* pitu*h*" iti | sa tu 'b*r*ihadvaso*h*' b*r*ihadvasur yasya tannâmakât pitur evâ 'dhyaish*t*a | "b*r*ihadvasur gobhilo gobhilât eva" iti | 'gobhilo' gobhilasyâ 'patya*m* 'b*r*ihadvasur' gobhilâd evâ 'dhîtavân [na] tv anyasmât | "gobhilo râdhâc ca gautamât" iti | gobhilo 'pi gotamasyâ 'patyât 'râdhat' etannâmakâd *r*isher vidyâta*h* samajani | eva*m* [d]vilaxa*n*â*m* *r*ishiparamparâ*m* darçayitvâ râdhâd gautamâd ârabhya va*m*ça*h* 'samânam' ity âha | samâna*m* para*m* samâna*m* param" iti | 'param' avaçish*t*am râdhâdi brahmaparyantam *r*ishijâtam "samânam" | abhyâsa âdarârtho brâhma*n*asamâptyarthaç ca |

|| Iti va*m*çabrâhma*n*abhâshye t*r*itîya*h* kha*nd*a*h* ||

|| Iti va*m*çabrâhma*n*abhâshya*m* samâptam ||

INDEX OF WORDS IN THE TEXT.

Proper names are in thick, parts of such names in spaced, and other words in ordinary type. The numbers refer to the sections. *Complete* proper names are given in the first case.

INDEX.

INDEX.

INDEX.

INDEX TO THE PREFACE.

A.

B.

C.

INDEX.

D.

E.

G.

H.

I.

J.

INDEX.

V.

W.

X.

Y.

Z.

Errata: p. vi., (last line but one) *read* Bombay As. Soc. J. ix. p. 10, line 4 from bottom, *read* adhitavân. p. 11., last line but one, *read* bâhvâ° *and* P. iv., 1, 96. Index, p. iv., ll. 4 and 5, *read* Nigada.

www.ingramcontent.com/pod-product-compliance
Lightning Source LLC
Chambersburg PA
CBHW021531270326
41930CB00008B/1194
9783741142338